*Concerning the
Eternal Predestination
of God*

Concerning the Eternal Predestination of God

JOHN CALVIN

Translated and with an Introduction
by J.K.S. Reid

Westminster John Knox Press
Louisville, Kentucky

First published 1961 by James Clarke & Co., Cambridge

Published in the U.S.A. 1997 by
Westminster John Knox Press, Louisville, Kentucky

Cover design by Jennifer K. Cox
Cover art by Antonio M. Rosario

This book is printed on acid-free paper that meets the
American National Standards Institute Z39.48 standard. ♾

PRINTED IN THE UNITED STATES OF AMERICA
97 98 99 00 01 02 03 04 05 06 — 10 9 8 7 6 5 4 3 2 1

Library of Congress Cataloging-in-Publication Data

Calvin, Jean, 1509–1564.
[De aeterna praedestinatione Dei. English]
Concerning the eternal predestination of God / John
Calvin ; translated and with an introduction by J.K.S. Reid.
  p.   cm.
ISBN 0-664-25684-8 (alk. paper)
1. Predestination—Early works to 1800. I. Reid, John
Kelman Sutherland. II. Title.
BT810.C2213   1997   96-49120
234'.9—dc21

EDITOR'S PREFACE

THE *De aeterna Praedestinatione Dei* was published at Geneva by John Crispin in 1552; but the intention which led to its appearance has its roots nine years earlier. Calvin's work *De libero Arbitrio* is dated 1543. As he himself states in the present work, the earlier book aimed at the refutation of the doctrine concerning Free Will put forward by Albert Pighius. This implacable disputant had no less vigorously contended against Calvin's doctrine of Predestination; but Calvin's undertaking to deal with this second part of his attack was delayed because of other pressing concerns. But the controversy about Predestination, so far from subsiding, broke out afresh, and Jerome Bolsec, formerly a monk and now a Protestant physician (though afterwards he reverted to Rome), repudiated Calvin's doctrine. Calvin rose in its defence. In October 1551, he charged Bolsec before the Genevan City Council (see *Actes du Procès* intenté par Calvin et les autres Ministres de Genève à Jérome Bolsec de Paris, preceding the *De aet. Praed.* in the same volume of *Corpus Reformatorum*), with some difficulty won his case, and secured the banishment of Bolsec and the vindication of his own doctrine. But Calvin judged that the harm done to the doctrine, and perhaps also to his own position, by Bolsec's criticism was not sufficiently remedied by the judicial condemnation of one chief opponent. There were besides him others, among them Georgius the Sicilian, named and briefly characterised in the present work. Moreover, behind these present opponents, Calvin saw the malign influence of Pighius with whom he had never fully dealt. It is this combination of circumstances that occasions the composition of the *De aeterna Praedestinatione*. In this one work, Calvin redeems an earlier promise to refute the views of Pighius about Predestination, though their exponent was no longer alive; he engages a living antagonist in the person of Georgius; and he deals with the continuing influence of Bolsec, though he is not named in the treatise. For the rest, the historical circumstances of the writing are sufficiently expounded in the course of the argument.

The passage of the work towards authorisation was, apparently, not entirely simple. Correspondence with Beza and Bullinger shows that advice was offered about its composition, and it looks as though the advice was taken. On 21st January 1552, the archives of the Genevan Senate record that the work was submitted to them, with the request for its authorisation in printed form. After scrutiny, the request was granted, and, as the introduction provided by *Corpus Reformatorum* maintains, a private writing of Calvin became an authentic document of Genevan orthodoxy, though it never enjoyed magisterial approval in the other Swiss states.

It appears that the French version followed the Latin original almost immediately—a translation which permitted itself a certain amount of freedom. The judgment expressed in *C R* is that it is not by the hand of Calvin himself, but by an amanuensis whose work Calvin invigilated and polished. Only one copy of this was accessible to the compilers of *C R*, and this is referred to in the footnotes as "the French copy" or more briefly as "French". The footnotes also record variations in the Latin text occurring in the reprints of Gallars (latiné Gallasius), Beza, Stoerius, Amsterdam and Niemeyer. Of these a little more information is obtainable in *C R*, vol. XXXVI (of Calvin's Works, vol. VIII), from which the translation that follows is made.

LIST OF CONTENTS

Concerning the Eternal Predestination of God

1. Formal Considerations

CALVIN is more widely known for his doctrine of Predestination than for any other belief which he held. This is regrettable for more than one reason. Those who know him only or primarily as author of this doctrine will certainly fail to appreciate him as theologian. For the theologian can in fact be assessed only when it is realised that, alongside of a God who for His glory apportions equally the lot of both the redeemed and the rejected, there is also represented a God of grace; and that it is Calvin's delight to set forth God in this light and his custom to do so at much greater length. Moreover, not only the theologian but also the theologian's system will be misapprehended, unless the place which the doctrine of Predestination occupies is carefully observed. For the opinion may be hazarded that, contrary to a prevalent view, the doctrine of Predestination by no means determines the system. Though it is indeed attached to and even integrated into the system, the part it plays is not really dominant; and there are points, for example where Calvin treats of the Church and of the sacraments, where it seems really supplementary to the main theme, and strictly dispensable. But of course little of this appears in the present work.

The treatise *Concerning the Eternal Predestination of God* is the longest and most sustained exposition which Calvin wrote on the subject. For those who wish to know what he holds, it supplies indispensable insight. A statement of his position is also to be found elsewhere, especially in the relevant parts of the *Institutes*. In the present treatise we have more than a bare statement. There is offered an extensive defence against the criticisms and contrary doctrines of those who chiefly opposed Predestination in Calvin's own day. In defending his doctrine, Calvin also necessarily expounds it further.

But, however important the treatise may be, it is not altogether easy to read and comprehend. The reason for this is the fact just mentioned. Calvin is concerned not only to set forth what he himself holds, but also to demolish contrary views. Thus he does not have before him a clear field through which he may pick his way unimpeded, but a field strewn with obstacles of his opponents' devising. To pursue the metaphor further, he is unable to advance continuously, but must ever and again retrace his footsteps when confronted with a barrier, in order to bring up the means by which it may be overcome. It often happens that a means of which he has earlier made use is again of help and value; and when this is the case, he does not scruple to summon it again to his assistance. For example, the *O homo, tu quis es?* of Rom 9.20 is repeatedly advanced' in the course of the argument, and almost as frequently there is adduced in various forms Augustine's affirmation that God's grace does not find but makes men elect. It is this that more than anything else imparts to the structure of Calvin's argument a character best described as laminated. Once this is frankly realised, much of the formal difficulty of his argument is resolved, and the circularity and repetitiveness which seem to characterise it are seen to give it added strength.

A further formal comment is perhaps called for. It is not now customary in theological controversy to label one's opponents dogs, or to depreciate their criticisms as barking, and so on. To find Calvin doing this and similar things with the greatest of gusto must strike the modern reader as strange and rather offensive. The translator is here confronted with a dilemma. To render such terms literally is to invite unfavourable comparison with the more courteous tone in which theological debates are today conducted. On the other hand, to mollify the expressions would be to debilitate the original and seriously to reduce its pungency. The first alternative has been deliberately adopted here. Two things may be said in explanation and extenuation of the choice. The first is that Calvin, as he himself says in his introduction, was singled out for vicious and even scurrilous criticism, which his initial composure in face of it did nothing to allay; and he also felt, with apparent right, that by these attacks the Church was being molested and injured. Thus both personal interest and concern for the Church combined to make a sharp rejoinder excusable. Secondly, when at last thus goaded to retort, Calvin simply used the kind of coin then current, and the terms employed by his opponents were even less restrained than his.

2. STATEMENT

2.1. Order

Calvin affirms that there is clearly a difference of condition amongst those who have a common nature. In the darkness common to all, some are illumined, while others remain blind. The question Calvin raises is how this differentiation comes about. His answer to the question is equally clear: we must confess that "God, by His eternal goodwill, which has no cause outside itself, destined those whom He pleased to salvation, rejecting the rest; those whom He dignified by gratuitous adoption, He illumined by His Spirit, so that they receive the life offered in Christ, while others voluntarily disbelieve, so that they remain in darkness destitute of the light of faith" (§I).

The two chief opponents whom Calvin has in mind have themselves much in common, though they differ in the details of what they severally hold. They too, on Calvin's showing, acknowledge the distinction between those who believe the Gospel and others who remain unbelieving. The difference, however, they think not to arise from God's free election or His secret counsel. It lies rather within the freedom of each man whether he is partaker of the grace of adoption or not; and accordingly each determines by his own will either the state of election for himself or that of reprobation (§I). Within this area of agreement, the differences between the two opponents are in principle small. Pighius in the main is concerned to maintain that, while the benefits of election are universally offered, the wicked deprive themselves of them independently of the will and counsel of God (§I). Georgius, on the other hand, is disposed to hold to universalism, while maintaining that the offer of salvation is on the evidence of Scripture made upon the basis not of election but of belief, not to the elect but to believers (§IX.8).

The point at issue between Calvin and his opponents is thus simple, but it is of course fundamental. Substantially what they do is to wrest the ground of salvation out of God's own hand where alone, Calvin holds, it rightly belongs, and to deposit it within the contingent realm of human volition and freewill. Clearly this is to derogate from the sovereignty of God. Here the doctrine of Predestination makes obvious contact with Calvin's general theological system. Since Predestination is an aspect of God's sovereignty, this by itself would be reason enough for Calvin to contend against the opponents of Predestination. There is no doubt that the injury done to the divine sovereignty, which Calvin sees implied in the denial of Predestination, is the reason for the resolution which characterises his positive assertions and the sharpness with which he denies those of his opponents. But it is typical of Calvin's approach and of his treatment of the subject that his chief and most frequent argument throughout the treatise should have a different form. He does not in the main object to his opponents: You cannot hold what you do, for this would be to injure the sovereignty of God. What he rather says is this: You cannot hold what you do, because it inverts the order of things as attested in Scripture and expounded in orthodox Christian tradition especially as exemplified by St Augustine. Thus referring to St Paul, he declares that he "expressly secures priority for God; for by His calling He causes them to begin to love Him who could do nothing but hate" (§V.1). Or again, alluding to Acts 13.48, he points out that St Paul, as recorded by Luke, asserts that ordination to eternal life takes precedence of belief (§VIII.1). St Augustine is just as clear and just as insistent that this is the order of things. He will not say (qtd §IV) that those who believe are chosen, but rather that they are chosen in order to believe. Or again, in even briefer terms (§V.3), grace does not find but makes men elect. Similarly, when Calvin expresses his own opinion without strict reference to scriptural or patristic terms, it is this certain order that he is concerned to affirm. Salvation, he says (§V.1), is based on election, and election in turn is based on God's gratuitous good pleasure. Or again, in a more circular form of expression (§VIII.6), election is followed by illumination by the Spirit in accordance with the will of God, and this in turn by faith, which is found in those who are elect. Or once more (§VIII.1), Calvin denies that there is anything in man himself which can accommodate or make a point of contact for illumination; no— the Spirit is the spirit of adoption, and this is purely gratuitous. It is not bestowed upon all, nor upon those who manifest faith; rather those upon whom it is bestowed have faith, and faith is thus the gift that ratifies election. The same insistence upon the correct order of things appears at another point, when Calvin takes up the matter of the order of the divine decrees (§VIII.5). He makes the Augustinian affirmation in negative form, that those who perish are not found but made worthy of destruction. This, he maintains, is consequent upon God's ordinances which follow in order thus: first, the determination of the destiny of the human race as a whole and as individuals; second, the appointment of Adam to death on account of his defection; and third, the condemnation of his posterity in him, except for those who are gratuitously elected out of the consequential entail.

The importance of this preoccupation with order can hardly be exaggerated. The matter of Predestination involves the nature of the relationship between several closely interdependent ideas: creator and creature, man's will and determinism, ground and cause, guilt and punishment, and so on. To define the order between such ideas is the same thing as to define their relationship. When therefore Calvin sets out the order that exists, he is not reducing the question to a logical abstraction. He is rather penetrating to the essence of the question, which, because it is a matter of relations, can most simply and clearly be stated in terms of logical order.

It is in this sense that Calvin is rightly said to be logical. A good deal of nonsense is talked about Calvin, as though his system were logical in the sense of being rounded off and complete; and the statement by frequent repetition has become almost a commonplace. In fact his system has not this character at all. It is certainly logical in the sense that the argument moves carefully step by step from one point to the next. But, to do it justice, it must be recognised as including elements not easily (or at all) capable of being harmonised—a *complexio oppositorum*, as H. Bauke says of it (see J. T. McNeill, *The History and Character of Calvinism*, Oxford University Press, New York, 1954, p. 202). Of special relevance to the purpose here is the following example. Pighius objects to Calvin that the dominical command to preach the Gospel universally conflicts with the doctrine of special election (§VIII.1). Calvin's brief answer to this conundrum is that Christ was ordained for the salvation of the whole world in such a way that only those who hear are saved. The universality of the grace of Christ is symbolised by a promiscuous preaching of the Gospel; the universality of the Mediator is paralleled by the universality of the call to penitence and faith. But at this point the harmony ends: the offer of salvation is made equally to all, but salvation itself is for those who are elect. It is the bare bones of the argument, then, that are exposed, even if the result manifests a certain awkward untidiness. There is no attempt to compel harmony or to systematise by force. That there is a consequent practical difficulty is obvious; and it is one which, whatever Calvin thought of it, was compelling enough to drive his opponents into another camp. The situation for Calvin is not really significantly relieved by what he adds to the argument. The universal offer of the Gospel does indeed have a meaning for those in whose case it is not effective. Quoting St Paul, Calvin says that for them it can only be a "savour of death unto death". The logicality of the exposition is so far preserved that the universal offer of salvation has at least some effective consequence in all cases. But the parallelism on analysis is found to be specious; the awkward untidiness reappears at a different point. It does not now consist in the fact that the same offer of the Gospel sometimes has and sometimes has not an effect; it now consists in the fact that it sometimes has an effect commensurable with its nature and with the purpose with which God designed it, and that sometimes, on the other hand, it has a quite opposite effect, incommensurable with its nature and the saving purpose of God—it precipitates death instead of life, destruction in place of salvation. This goes to show that Calvin's first loyalty is directed, not to formal adherence to abstract logicality, but to the facts of the case and situation as he conceived them, or rather as he conceived the Scriptures to depict them. The logicality of his thought is dedicated not to the formation of a system, but rather to the eliciting of the meaning and the implications of those facts which, as it seemed to him, belong to the body of Christian truth.

2.2. Foreknowledge

In emphasising the order of things which alone represents the truth, Calvin has outlined the principle governing his understanding of Predestination. It remains to fill in this outline, and this he does for the most part in answer to the objections and contrary views which Pighius and others advance. One of the earliest and most contentious matters to be treated is the divine foreknowledge. On Pauline authority, Predestination is linked with God's foreknowledge: those are predestined whom God foreknew. Both Calvin and his opponents acknowledge this, but the connotation given to the term knowledge is different in each case. His opponents allege that what St Paul means is that each is elected in view of his faith which God foresees—a doctrine which the Arminians were later to profess and hold against Calvinism. Calvin's reply is that "no one denies that it was foreknown by God who were to be heirs of eternal life" (§V.1). But the object of God's foreknowledge is not what the elect will be in themselves but precisely what He Himself will make of them. Positively, the faith and repentence which are found in the elect are themselves a gift of God, and not a virtue to be first displayed before election takes place. Negatively, the election of God cannot wait upon the fulfilling of such an indeterminate condition. It is once more a question of order: election is prior to faith and repentence, and not dependent upon them. Besides, Calvin makes use of the more intimate meaning of knowledge which is certainly biblical and which he finds expressed especially in the Psalms and the Fourth Gospel: the way of the righteous is known to God; I know my sheep. For his opponents, election is dependent upon knowledge; for Calvin, election and knowledge are in the last resort identical.

2.3. God's reason in election

Closely connected with what has just been said is the question of God's reason in election. Pighius is in a position to suggest such a reason. It is, he says, the foreseen faith of those who are then elected; and Calvin, denying this reason, seems to make election sheerly incomprehensible. Calvin's retort is (§VIII.4) that he nowhere says that God's counsel is without reason. On the contrary, he denies both the reason Pighius suggests, and also that God is moved fortuitously in what He does. This he does in order to maintain that God's counsel has indeed a reason which is both admirable and incomprehensible. However hidden it may be, we may safely say that His reason is the glory of His name. Calvin here willingly embraces what Pighius calls a contradiction, and is content both to deny that the reason may be sought and to teach what that reason is.

A negative consideration is added. If faith is the reason for God's election, it is clearly a reason external to Himself. Grace then may be held to be offered to all equally, and in the last resort it is by the will of men, as each is willing to receive it, that it is rendered efficacious (§V.2). This amounts to saying that the elect are saved by Christ, provided that they look after themselves (§VIII.6). But this constitutes an intolerable insult to Christ. For He Himself affirms that His protection is invincible, promises to give eternal life to all given Him by the Father, and teaches that the elect are in His hands from which nothing can pluck them out. If then the reason for God's election is to be found in man, or anywhere else than wholly and simply in God Himself, injury is done to the efficacy of Christ's work. It has to be supplemented before it becomes efficacious. The question may indeed quite properly be asked why God acts so (§VIII.4); and to this question, the answer is: because He willed. But any supplementary enquiry why He so willed is to ask for something greater and higher than the will of God itself; and this is to ask for what is not.

Similar considerations apply to the relations of God's grace and man's will. Pighius maintains that man's will may not be left out of account. Negatively he declares that the cause of reprobation is the rejection of calling. In reply, Calvin appeals to Scripture (§VIII.12). There we find it written that it is not of him that wills, nor of him that runs, but of God that shows mercy. This alone might refute Pighius' opinion. But there is in fact something in what he says, and Calvin, it turns out, is not disposed to deny that man's will enters into the matter of his salvation. It is indeed a factor. But the part it plays has to be carefully observed. If it were an independent factor alongside of the mercy of God, then we should have to say that the mercy of God was not alone sufficient, unless the consent of our will is antecedently supplied. But here a false equality has obtruded itself, and the right priorities have been obscured. God's mercy is shown not when it is found that we will. The order is: if God have mercy, then we will. For it is God that works in us both to will and to do. No one can deny that a good will is the gift of God Himself. Thus the will without which indeed salvation is not obtainable is consequent upon and not conditional for the operation of the mercy or grace of God.

Calvin thus retracts the whole operation of election into the hands of God. Even the loophole provided by the suggestion that God finds the reason for what is admittedly His action in something extrinsic to Himself is stopped. Reason God certainly has, but it too is to be found within Himself.

2.4. Reprobation

The best way of expounding what Calvin has to say about the shadow side of the doctrine of Predestination, that is about reprobation, will be to note carefully and in some detail what is said in one chief passage where he deals with the matter. In general, Calvin, like Augustine before him, is much more disposed to talk about election than about reprobation, and has certainly more to say about it. Moreover, at a crucial point in the argument, it is analogy with God's action in election that plays a decisive role for defining His action in reprobation. This should be borne in mind when assessing Calvin's doctrine as a whole. Reprobation is of course an essential part of his doctrine of Predestination; but it is rather less than dominant, and the prominence it has is because it tends to stick up like a sore finger.

Calvin considers the passage Is 6.9 (§V.5): Hear indeed and do not understand; see indeed but do not perceive. The blindness of which the prophet here speaks is in a sense attributable to the prophet; but the part played by him is clearly accidental and may be disregarded. The blindness may be attributed to the punishment which God inflicts; and this in turn leads back to the unbelief which certainly preceded the blindness and of which it may be supposed to be the divine requital. But, Calvin argues, in effect, the establishment of this causal connection would prove too much. The fact is that, though all are afflicted by unbelief, some nevertheless are delivered from it, granted illumination, and brought to salvation. Hence another aspect of the question opens up: it must be asked how, out of the common condition of unbelief, some are recovered and saved. The answer which human standards would suggest, says Calvin, is that the cause is to be found in the individuals themselves. This is indeed true up to a point; but it is not a complete answer. For God does not permit us to stop there. It is grace that saves out of the common defection; that is, it is the work of God.

The insight thus achieved from examination of the positive side of the doctrine of Predestination is now employed in the case of the negative side, that is of reprobation. If unbelief in and by itself were the ground of reprobation, it would thereby be accorded a status equal to grace; for as grace occasioned the salvation of some, so unbelief would occasion the loss of others. This in turn would imply that unbelief (or wickedness, for Calvin uses the terms as alternatives here) must be thought of as contending on equal terms with grace and as being stronger than it. As he puts it in other words (§VIII.2), the will of God would be overpowered by weak man—the weakness of man would be stronger than the strength of God, and God's omnipotence would be forfeit.

But Scripture shows the way out of this dilemma. The divine mercy is not to be put on an equality with the wickedness of men; nor is any struggle between the two contemplated. God's mercy, on the testimony of Scripture, lights upon whom He will, not merely upon whom He can, that is on those who are otherwise eligible. The truth about reprobation is expressed by the affirmation that is complementary to this: and whom He wills He hardens.

The ground for reprobation is thus complex. It is quite correct to say that unbelief or wickedness is its cause; but it is not right to say that it is the sole cause. The argument leads to a deeper cause or ground: if men's unbelief or wickedness is their own responsibility, nevertheless that they remain in that state is due to the secret counsel of God. So the gracious doctrine of Predestination is completed by the addition of a more forbidding aspect, and election is supplemented by reprobation. Whatever may be said about the causal conditions with which these high concepts are connected, they are at least both alike in this, that for the ultimate cause or ground of each we cannot stop short at any merely human or temporal factor, however indispensable it may be as condition, but must trace the matter in the case of each of them back into the ultimately hidden recesses of the counsel of God. Of reprobation, just as of election, we may say that its cause is laid up there, even if we cannot say what it is, beyond appealing to the glory of the divine name.

2.5. *Election, reprobation and justice*

Calvin realises that what has been said about election and reprobation raises some difficulty when the justice of the procedure is considered. The difficulty is in two parts. There is first the simple question whether, if reprobation is thus grounded in God Himself, what is done is really just. Calvin's reply (§VIII.5) is to affirm uncompromisingly the liability of man. The reprobate are justly left in death, for in Adam they are all dead and condemned; it is just that the children of wrath should perish. Adam himself was created perfectly righteous, and he fell by his own will. By this fall, Adam involves the whole race in a similar all-inclusive liability. It is true that Adam's fall and the consequent sinful acts of his posterity may not be said to be done without God's ordination. The fact is, as Augustine says, that what is done against God's will is not done without God's will. But it by no means follows that God is the author of sin. Calvin is at pains to repeat several times that the proper and genuine cause of sin is not God's hidden counsel, but the will of man. God's ordination is not an ineluctable necessity, whatever it may be. Between His ordination and sin there stands the proximate cause of sin which is man's will. The intervention of this proximate cause on the one hand removes all guilt from God, and on the other hand leaves man with a liability which he cannot escape. Men therefore, justly incur eternal loss, and no one has cause to complain of an unjust severity on the part of God.

The second part of the difficulty is more complex. Calvin admits that at first glance the mind is disturbed to hear of grace denied to some who are quite unworthy, while it is granted to others who are equally unworthy. His answer to this is itself in two parts (§VIII.5). He is first of all concerned to show that this is at least a permissible inequality of treatment. He uses for this purpose a human analogy borrowed from Augustine. A human creditor, he says, is quite entitled to exact a debt from one of his debtors and to remit it in the case of another. This then, may be taken for a simile and applied to the relations of God and man. God, too, is entitled, since all are His debtors, to remit or to exact as He wills. But there remains the residual question why there should in fact be such disparity of treatment. Calvin seems to admit that the disparity in the human case is indeed inequitable. But here the analogy breaks down, and we may not apply the metaphor to God. The divine justice is not to be measured by human justice. We may not impose upon God any restriction at all in having mercy on whom He will. Any protest must be immediately silenced by the *O homo, tu quis es?* We have, in other words, simply to marvel at the profundity of the judgments of God; and this concludes all disputations.

Calvin therefore, enjoins that curiosity should be curbed. But for further assurance and to allay all suspicion about the justice of what God does, he adds another consideration. Borrowing again from Augustine, he bids us take a larger view. God who created all things foreknew that evil would arise out of this good creation. But He also knew how to make good out of this evil; and He deemed it more appropriate to His omnipotent goodness to effect this good than not to allow evil at all. For this reason, He ordained the life of men and angels to show first what this freewill could do, and then what by His justice and grace He could effect.

Two things are thus made apparent. The justice of God is, in Calvin's view, fully vindicated, and the culpable guilt of men is demonstrated. The summary of the matter cannot be better given than in Calvin's own words. "The ungodly", he says (§IX.7), "who voluntarily provoke the wrath of God upon themselves, were before divinely reprobated by a cause which was just though unknown."

2.6. The doctrine to be preached

In the *Institutes*, Calvin is very frank about the solemnising character of the doctrine he is led to propound. Yet he is in no doubt that, tremendous and awesome (*horribile*) though it is, it must be declared and proclaimed. In the present treatise, there is a rather different emphasis. He does not so frankly acknowledge the solemnity of the doctrine, but with even greater stress he repeatedly affirms the need to preach it. The sufficient reason for its being proclaimed is that this is done in Scripture. Scripture gives us the definition of Predestination and also the precept that it be declared; and of this the apostle Paul is the outstanding example.

The purpose of preaching this doctrine is the banishment of indolence in believers. Here the preaching of the doctrine plays the same part as the believer's assurance. It is given, not that they can then lie down and fall asleep, but that they may be stirred up to depend wholly on God for their security, to enjoy their assurance, and to watch with prayer. The indolence of the flesh is rebuked by the preaching of God's electing grace (§VIII.8).

The effect of such preaching is twofold. The appeal is

addressed equally to the elect and the reprobate; but its effect is different, and appropriate to each case. As the office *proprium* of the Gospel is salvation, but its office *accidentale* is the rejection of the Gospel with attendant reprobation, so too with the preaching of Predestination which is an essential part of the Gospel. Even the elect do not always follow the right course, and they are properly bidden to take care lest they perish, to engage in perpetual conflict, and to be constantly vigilant. The effect upon the ungodly is that, though obdurate in their evil, they may yet be pricked by such a stimulus. Thus, though they are not effectively turned from their condition, yet they are given warning of it, so that they are without excuse (§IX.6).

Certain limits are prescribed for the preaching of the doctrine. The first is a temporal limitation. The doctrine is to be proclaimed in simple obedience to our Lord's command until the day of revelation comes. The second concerns the audience to which the preaching is to be addressed. Proclamation is to be made to all, since the doctrine is deposited with us for this end, until the obstinacy of the unbelievers blocks the way. The third limitation prescribes the way in which the preaching is to be carried out. Here Calvin borrows again from Augustine. Two implications which might be drawn from the doctrine are fallacious and illegitimate, and they may not play a part in its proclamation. The conclusion may not be drawn or employed: if you do not believe, it is because you are destined by God to destruction. This would be merely the expression of malice and an excuse for idleness on the part of the preacher. Nor may implications be drawn for the future, by saying that those who hear never will believe because they are reprobate. This would be imprecation rather than doctrine (§IX.7).

2.7. Assurance

The final word in a statement of Calvin's doctrine should refer to the fine and impregnable sense of assurance which the doctrine imparts to the believer. This comes to such repeated expression throughout the treatise, that little requires to be said about it here. The Fourth Gospel is especially drawn upon to convey this sense of certainty. On dominical authority it is said that the Father gives Christ the sheep that are His, that the Father is greater than all, and that these sheep can therefore never be plucked from His hand. Those whose present and

future remain in the custody of the Father have and enjoy an
inviolable security.

3. EXPOSITORY COMMENT

3.1. Man's responsibility

While the ground of Predestination is securely and unambiguously located in the divine ordination, it is at the same
time Calvin's clear intention in the treatise to vindicate human
responsibility. To show this, it is again necessary to refer to
various sections of the treatise, since, as has been said, the
development of the theme is determined rather fortuitously by
the contrary views which Calvin contests. In what he has to say
on this issue, there are three steps discernible, though this is to
systematise what is said rather more than Calvin himself does,
and each of these calls for some attention.

First of all, the voluntary character of man's sinful action
is established. The crucial passage (§VIII.5) is where Calvin
seeks to vindicate the justice of God in leaving the reprobate to
the death and destruction which they incur by their unbelief.
The argument leads him to specify the case of the first man,
Adam. What is said applies equally to Adam's posterity, since
they inherit from him their lost condition. Adam, however, falls
not without the knowledge and ordination of God. Yet this
neither mitigates his guilt nor involves God in any blame. The
reason for this is that, though the ordination of God is involved
in the fall, nevertheless the fall comes about by Adam's own
will. Calvin reiterates with emphasis: we must always remember
that he voluntarily deprived himself of the rectitude he had
received from God, voluntarily gave himself to the service of
sin and Satan, and voluntarily precipitated himself into
destruction. In Calvin's mind, divine ordination in no way
conflicts with the voluntary and therefore culpable character
of human wrongdoing.

One consideration may be urged by way of excuse and so of
exculpation of Adam and his posterity. What if there was no
possibility of his evading this ordination of God? Calvin
dismisses this suggestion summarily. If, he says, the action is
done voluntarily, this is enough to establish his guilt. It is
indeed more than enough; for what he calls the proper and
genuine cause of sin lies in the will of man, and it is therefore idle
to look elsewhere for its cause, with the intention of diverting

culpability to another quarter. To make use of the term which we should now normally use, man is responsible in his sinning.

3.2. Man is knowingly responsible

Calvin does not leave the matter there. Man is not only responsible in some logical but unapprehended sense; he is in fact knowingly responsible. Calvin is aware (§VI) that there is apparent absurdity or contradiction in affirming both the voluntary character of the fall and also its ordination by the counsel of God. There is, however, a factor which cannot be ignored and which must in this matter be accorded precedence. "Over against a thousand witnesses", he says, "the voice of conscience ought to suffice for us." In face of the evidence which it supplies, we should be ashamed to deny that man perishes justly for preferring to follow Satan rather than God. To put it in other words which Calvin also uses, there is an "internal sense" (§VII), or more specifically an "internal feeling of the heart" (loc. cit.), or again a "sense of sin" (§VIII.5); and this is so engraved upon the hearts of men as never to be entirely lost. His own conscience condemns a man; and it follows from this that any attempt to absolve himself is the work of impiety.

In another passage (§IX.7), Calvin declares that the sins a man commits must be imputed by him to himself. Adam may not plead the solicitation of Eve as excuse for what he does; for the poison of infidelity is to be found within himself. Nor may man evade his own responsibility by tracing back into the recesses of the hidden counsels of God the cause of the sin that he commits, since the cause of the sin is to be found nearer at home in his own heart. These attempted evasions are not only ineffective. They are known to be ineffective; for man is too strongly bound by the chains of conscience to free himself from the condemnation which he incurs.

Summarising, we may say that in Calvin's view the voluntary character of sin is the *ratio essendi* of man's culpability, while the sense of sin or conscience is its perpetual and unavoidable *ratio cognoscendi*.

3.3. Proximate and remote causes

For mitigating some of the difficulty involved in affirming both man's responsibility and God's ordination, Calvin makes use of the distinction between proximate and remote causes. As already said, an "internal sense of their own mind" forces men to the conclusion that evil arises from the voluntary defection of the first man. More explicitly, if they look around in the attempt to divert the blame for sin to another quarter, they are prevented by the fact that its proximate cause resides within themselves, whereas it is only the remote cause that is to be traced to the divine ordination (§VII). Or again (§VIII.5), what Calvin calls the proper and genuine cause of sin is not God's hidden counsel, but the will of man. The point is emphasised by an illustration suggested by a fragment of the poet Ennius. Medea, for love of the stranger, Jason, betrays her country. They both flee to Corinth, where Jason deserts his accomplice in crime. This infidelity awakes her to a sense of her own perfidy; but what she immediately denounces is not herself, but the timber of the grove of Pelius which was hewn down to build the ship they had used. This the poet ridicules, for she is clearly seeking the cause of her misfortune in manifestly remote conditions, while the real cause is to be found within herself. So in the case of those who, seeking the cause of their sin and consequent ruin, break into the recesses of heaven, instead of listening to that internal sense which declares that the real cause is in themselves. A consideration of the distinction between proximate and remote causes corrects this self-deception. On the one hand, the distinction means that God is not the author of sin, and on the other it involves man in total culpability. It is in this way that Calvin settles the question of culpability or moral responsibility. Culpability attaches to the proximate cause of the sinful action, and is so completely absorbed by it that none remains over for attachment to the remote cause. This is the fact which it is the office of that "internal feeling of the heart" or "sense of sin" to endorse.

But Calvin seems also to be aware that there is a more metaphysical question that has not been fully answered. The matter can be put in this way. Does the relation between human causality and divine ordination leave room for a freedom in man sufficient to sustain the burden of blame? What if metaphysically the divine ordination, though only a remote cause, rendered the independence of the proximate cause so void that it became unable to be the bearer of moral blame? Calvin tackles this problem later in the treatise (§X.7). He begins by repeating that even the most fortuitous things are directed by the divine counsel. To support this statement, he quotes Prov

16.33: The lot is thrown into the lap, but the judgment of things is from the Lord; and also Ex 21.13, where Moses declares that it is God's purpose that the accidental blow of the axe should kill a man. The objection is alleged that this catches up everything into an iron necessity such as the Stoics propounded. Calvin repudiates the charge. The Stoic philosophy does indeed weave all causes into a kind of Gordian complex, just as the astrologers of the day hold that absolute necessity originates from the position of the stars. The doctrine of Predestination, however, has nothing to do with such a fateful necessity. God is not one among the number of causes and a link in the chain which they form. He disposes all things by His free will. Calvin is willing to conceive of two forms of necessity. It is true, he says, that what God freely decrees necessarily happens. But this is quite different from natural necessity, which is embedded in things in themselves; and at the same time, it is quite compatible with what we must call natural contingency. To illustrate the first point: it is true that God in the beginning commanded the earth to produce herbs and fruit, and this initially sufficed, without the intervention of human work. But now man is invited to work, and certainly must not expect to have bread by mere idle desire. God then makes the earth fruitful, but man must work. Similarly (§VIII.4) we may not deny that the day is created by God because it is also made by the splendour of the sun. As for the second point to be made, Calvin declares that the future is hidden from us, and we must at the same time trust the providence of God and also conduct our lives in view of the contingency of unknown things. We have therefore to conceive of two orders of necessity. There is the supernatural order which belongs to the divine ordination of all things. But besides this, there is the natural order, which may also in certain aspects be called an order of contingency. It is within this natural order that proximate causes have their place, and it is here in the case of man that the idea of culpability applies. That God is indeed the remote cause of all things as little removes culpability from the human agent as it destroys the reality of the natural order of necessity.

3.4. Predestination, determination and determinism

Something more may properly be said about these two orders just mentioned, though what will now be said goes a little beyond what Calvin explicitly states. Predestination is not the same as determination, and it is even more widely different from determinism. By determination is meant the influencing of the conduct of something in a greater or less degree by certain factors or conditions, one or more, external or internal. Determinism is the hardening of this conception into a mechanical compulsion by factors operating strictly *a tergo*, so that what is done is the exact and necessary consequence of those antecedent factors. Calvin's Predestination has really nothing to do with antecedent factors—not even with factors earlier than those involved in determination. It has to do with factors, or more strictly with a factor, if the term be admissible at all, which is prior to antecedence of any kind, and it is therefore located not at an earliest point in time but rather pretemporally or supratemporally. While the other terms operate within the temporal category and are thus definable, Predestination has a non-temporal character which constitutes it another order of being. Predestination or predetermination is not determination simply by a greater power, but is different in kind from mere determination and hence *a fortiori* from determinism. Predestination is quite different from fate. It follows that while determination raises an acute problem with regard to human responsibility, Predestination does not necessarily do so. Indeed, so far from being incompatible with such independence as is required to establish responsibility, it is itself the concept under which this independence can (to put it so) carve out for itself a real place. Philosophically, when we deal with the relation of a finite magnitude to a greater but also finite magnitude, the independence of the one is conserved only at the expense of the other; when we deal with a really infinite magnitude and its relation to a finite magnitude, this is no longer the case. Theologically, God is not simply the magnification of man, and His qualities are not simply the qualities of man increased to the power of n. If this were true of Him, then predetermination would be merely determination on a greater, grander scale, and there would be even less hope of securing the independence of the finite magnitude which man is. But just because He is really infinite, the Predestination of which He is the author does not rob man of his independence and therefore of his responsibility. Now it is really Predestination for which Calvin argues, and he must be deemed to be quite right in maintaining that man, though predetermined by the decrees of God, is yet secure in that degree of independence which permits of responsibility being attributed to him.

3.5. Freedom

It is notable that Calvin has very little to say about human freedom. This must strike the reader as perplexing, for it is customary in modern discussion of the subject to link freedom with responsibility so closely that the terms become virtually synonymous. The freedom thought of here is a freedom on the part of the moral agent either to do or not to do; it is a freedom of indeterminacy. But Calvin thinks of freedom quite differently. The freedom of which the Bible speaks, whether we look at what is said in Genesis or in St Paul, is not an indetermination of this kind. It is a positive freedom in doing the will of God. To put it in other words, it is equally a freedom for and a freedom from—a freedom for the service of God, resulting in a freedom from the things that would impede obedient service. The contradictory of this freedom is not determination as such, but rather the choice of evil which results in bondage to the powers of evil. This is the sense in which Luther so powerfully and insistently represented the distinction between the *libertas Christiani hominis* and the *servum arbitrium*. So too St Augustine distinguishes between *arbitrium* as choice and *voluntas* as will, holding that man has *voluntas*, but only when turned by grace towards the good does he make choice (*arbitrium*) of the good. It is in such theological terms that Calvin, too, conceives freedom. It is, moreover, a freedom which men in Adam have lost (see *Institutes*, 2.2), and which only Christ can restore (2.6). With the freedom of indeterminacy with which ethics deals he is therefore not concerned. It is enough for his purpose if he can show that men are responsible; and this is at least his intention.

3.6. God's part and man's

A further word may here be added to clarify what Calvin holds concerning the parts played respectively by God and by man. Pighius maintained that man is the arbiter of his future condition and has either fortune within his own hands; and he concludes that the discrimination between elect and reprobate cannot be determined by an eternal decree of God. It follows, as Calvin says, that God must await the outcome and final issue of a man's life in doubt and suspense. In the light of what has been said, it is clear that Pighius confuses two orders of necessity. He is indeed right up to a point: man does lead his own real life, in an order in which one thing naturally leads to another; and this is why he cannot evade culpability. But this, on Calvin's view, is quite compatible with his ordination by a divine decree which is the remote cause of what he does and which appoints the final issue to which all he does leads.

It is then entirely proper to speak of the responsible agency of man; but the phrase must be used with care. His responsible agency operates in the natural order. Error is immediately incurred if this order and this responsible agency are regarded as respectively co-ordinate with the divine order and the freedom with which God acts. Co-ordination of this kind implies interrelation or rather inter-operation: what each of the parties does is dependent upon what the other does. Calvin's emphasis on Predestination demands that no such correlation be admitted. On the contrary, dependence is strictly a one-way relation—man is dependent upon God and what he does on what God does, and not and never *vice versa*. This is the reason why he will not hear of two wills in God, why he rejects the distinction of the "sophists of the Sorbonne" between the regulative and the absolute will of God, why all such discriminations as the Arminians were to make between the absolute and the conditional will of God or between the executive and the permissive will of God had to be contradicted. He does indeed allow the concept of permission (§VIII.5). But he uses it with a carefully defined connotation. On the human side, he declares, what is done contrary to God's will is yet not done without His will, for His permitting or allowing it is the condition of its being done at all. On the divine side, however, this permission cannot be construed as a sort of capitulation to *force majeure*, nor even as indicating a necessary alteration or improvisation on the part of a will originally differently disposed. God's permission, says Calvin, is not unwilling but willing. Sometimes he goes so far in limiting the admissible idea of permission as to disallow its use altogether (§X.10, 11). "It is useless", he says, "to have recourse to the concept of permission", or to set up a distinction between what God does so that some things are done only by His permission. What he refers to here, as he makes clear, is an "otiose" or "quiescent" permission. The will of God, that is to say, is not only free, but also simple and eternal.

3.7. Calvin's intention

If Calvin's doctrine has been rightly expounded, what was stated at the beginning of this third section may be held to have been demonstrated. It is clearly his intention to vindicate and establish the full reality of human action. Within the doctrine of Predestination, man's solemn responsibility is secured. He is aware of at least many of the difficulties involved, but, whatever the appearances may be, and however we must finally judge the doctrine, he believes himself to have fulfilled this intention.

3.8. The place of Predestination in Calvin's system

The opening paragraph of this introduction expressed the doubt whether Predestination should be allowed the dominant place in Calvin's system commonly allotted to it. No more than a passing reference is permissible here, since the evidence for assessing the grounds of this doubt lie wholly outside the present work. A brief allusion to Calvin's doctrine of the Church and of the sacraments must suffice to show that the predominance of Predestination in Calvin's theology is certainly not unlimited.

As is now fairly generally realised, Calvin puts forward a high view of the Church. "Such is the effect of union with the Church, that it retains us in the fellowship of God" (*Institutes*, 4.1.3); negatively, "out of her bosom there can be no hope of remission of sins, or any salvation" (op. cit., 4.1.4). It is true that the idea of election makes an occasional appearance: "all the elect of God are so connected with each other in Christ, that, as they depend upon one head, so they grow up together as into one body" (op. cit., 4.1.3). But the introduction of the idea is irresolute. The fact is that logically the Church's membership and the membership of the elect should really coincide. Yet Calvin shrinks from making such a statement. So high is his view of the Church that the idea of Predestination is really thrust into the background.

Similarly with the sacraments. Calvin is concerned to show (*Institutes*, 4.14.9) that they do not possess a "perpetual inherent virtue, efficacious in itself", but that it is as instituted by God that they promote the "establishment and augmentation" of faith; and it is for the same reason that they "confer no advantage or profit without being received by faith" (op. cit., 4.14.16). But the efficacy that is accorded to them by God is so emphasised that the predestinarian thought that men are chosen in order that they may believe is hardly mentioned. Calvin never says that the sacraments are effectual in the case of the elect alone. Here then is one place at least where Predestination is not really geared into what Calvin says—a place, moreover, which is by no means unimportant in Calvin's eyes. This must be allowed to influence the judgment to be passed on the predominance of Predestination in the total system.

4. CRITICAL COMMENT

4.1. God's justice

Is Calvin's vindication of God's justice valid? Certain further questions arise which have to be faced at this point. The frequent use which Calvin makes of the *O homo, tu quis es?* can hardly be overlooked. Amplifying what St Paul says in the relevant passage in Romans, Calvin affirms that it is an axiom for both the apostle and all pious minds, and even for common sense, that "the inscrutable judgment of God is greater than men can penetrate" (§III). This is of course a paraphrase of the words of St Paul. One wonders, however, whether in so paraphrasing them Calvin does not read a more strictly judicial meaning into them than St Paul intends. It is true on the one hand that the reference is to Ps 36.6, and there the Hebrew parallelism connects judgments with righteousness. On the other hand, the parallelism which St Paul makes is between judgment and ways, and this suggests that a strictly judicial meaning is not read into the word judgment by him. In a later passage (§VIII.4), Calvin contends that to give one's will as the sole sufficient reason for an action is tyrannical in the case of men; but he denies that the principle can be applied to God without sacrilege. For us, the mere good pleasure of God is and must be an entirely sufficient reason: "God possesses such great power, that we ought to be content with His mere nod." He adds that the vengeance which God exacts upon the ungodly is more than just. Further, as has already been said, when challenged concerning the justice of the action of God in electing some and reprobating others, Calvin has recourse to the recesses of the hidden counsels of God (§VIII.5). Perhaps most explicit of all is Calvin's citation (loc. cit.) of Augustine to the effect that the divine justice is not to be measured by human justice.

Calvin's argument here has not allayed the uneasiness of all his readers, and the reason for this fact is worth examining. The question is whether it is possible to think of a justice in God which is greater than our justice. To say that God is greater than man needs no justification. As Isaiah says (55.8), "my thoughts are not your thoughts, neither are your ways my ways, saith the Lord". So long as this is intended in a metaphysical sense, no difficulty arises. Similarly of some of the moral attributes it may quite properly be said that God possesses them in greater degree than do we, and no one is likely to find difficulty in conceiving the love of God as greater than human love. But the attribute of justice is (as Aristotle affirms in his *Nicomachean Ethics*) in a special case, and does not so readily permit of greater and less degrees. No doubt we speak of a "larger justice". For justice is permitted a certain latitude in the means it employs. Besides the strict adherence to just principles, there is also the promotion of justice—the idea which the biblical understanding of righteousness includes. Justice may therefore use different instruments: by punishment, justice may be vindicated; but forgiveness, while not violating the canons of justice, may do even more to advance righteousness. When justice is thus placed in a wider context, it may therefore be conceived as "larger"; but at least it involves no injustice, and there are recognisable moral conditions which determine which means may be employed. It therefore differs in principle from what Calvin seems here to be arguing for. The selection of some for favour and the leaving of others to the ruin, which indeed they merit, but in no greater degree than those who are favoured, does appear to be inequitable. And the suspicion that there is here a violation of justice is not set at rest by appealing to a justice not to be measured by human justice. If our conception of justice is a reliable key to justice anywhere, to have recourse to the hidden counsels of God will not save that which seems to be unjust from really being so.

Is it possible that Calvin in fact is applying a metaphysical solution to what is really a moral problem? Does he here slip from the moral sphere where the problem has arisen over to the metaphysical sphere, without observing that a transition has been made? One of the phrases which he uses makes this appear likely. As already quoted, he represents God as possessing "such great power (*tantum potestatis*, not *talem potestatem*) as ought to content us" with the justice of what He does. That he is capable of making an error of this kind is supported by an argument used at another point (§VIII.2). He quotes with approval what Augustine has to say when he argues as follows. Augustine's real point is that man is quite unable to contribute anything to his own salvation. For, suppose the contrary. Man will then by exercise of his free will supply or withhold the condition upon which salvation becomes his. Since he is the creature of God, this freewill is God's gift; and, being free in the sense supposed, it may be used for either good or evil. Then the good will, that is freewill rightly used, is our own. Therefore, Augustine concludes, what we contribute is better than what comes from God.—The comment to be made, however, is that two things are being compared and assessed as better and worse respectively which in fact are incommensurable, since they belong to different categories. A freewill committed in a good direction is certainly qualifiable as good. But a freewill as it *ex hypothesi* comes from God in an uncommitted state cannot properly be qualified by moral attributes at all. As the gift of God, it may be good in a general way, but as uncommitted it is not good in any strictly moral way. It is true that Augustine makes a bluff retort to this reasoning. Man, he says, is himself unable to invest anything with goodness; how then could his use of freewill make it for the first time good in a moral sense? Rather, he would say, all the gifts of God are good, and freewill as one of them must be deemed good too. But this form of reply would only underline and corroborate what is being said. Augustine is here carelessly passing from the metaphysical realm to the moral; and, the suggestion is, Calvin too readily follows him at this point.

Perhaps too much stress should not be put upon this apparent transposition of key. It is after all an *argumentum ad hominem* that Calvin adopts in order to show up the faulty reasoning of an opponent. But it certainly does nothing to dispose of the suspicion that at a more crucial place in the argument, Calvin does confuse the metaphysical and the moral.

4.2. Symmetry

How are the decrees of salvation and of reprobation related to one another, and how are they each related to the will of God? Calvin's arguments are deployed over against the contentions of Pighius and others. It is in the context of the thesis that the whole human race is chosen, so that whoever lays hold upon Christ by faith obtains salvation (§V.1), that Calvin makes one of the clearest statements in the matter. There is, he says, "a mutual relation between the elect and the reprobate"; the concept of election remains coherent so long as we suppose that "God separated out from others certain men as seemed good to Him". There is, that is to say, a radical distinction between two classes, those who are elect and those who are reprobate. Those classes are equal in status, and at the same time are mutually exclusive. Both experience and Scripture make this distinction apparent. Common sense tells us that salvation is not obtained by all. To this, Scripture adds its witness; for in the Old Testament it appears that God's law is not proclaimed to the Gentiles, and God does not will His truth to be known by them (§VIII.2). The particularity of calling which is apparent in the Old Testament and declared in the New is a principle that still operates. The distinction between the some that are elect and the others who are reprobate is absolute. This difference between the two classes has to be accounted for and the cause of the distinction established. Pighius' view is that the cause of the distinction is to be found in man. Choice is what distinguishes between man and his neighbour, between those that are saved and those that are lost. For man is "the arbiter of his future condition and has either fortune in his hand". Faith obtains the salvation proffered, whereas unbelief must forfeit it (§VI). The condition of all men is the same. The element that enters in to determine a difference of destiny is man's own conduct; and some, though like the others they were elected, by their failure deprive themselves of eternal life (§V.3).

Calvin's retort consists first in an appeal to Scripture. The argument of Pighius commends itself to common sense and to natural judgment. But the fact is that it is not this common-sense reason that St Paul employs in his account. Instead, he traces back the distinction to a more profound level and finds it grounded in the ordination of God. That is to say, when it would have been easy for him to account for the distinction between the true and the spurious children of God by the simple presence or absence of the mark of faith, he deliberately raises the question to the level of divine election. The distinction is not of human contrivance but of divine ordination (§V.3).

A corollary follows. On Pighius' view the distinction between the saved and the lost is grounded in a difference of human action or response. He can thus maintain the integrity of God's disposition and attitude. Being Himself willing that all should come to salvation, His will is disposed identically towards all men. But Calvin's representation of the matter implies a difference within the will of God. The differentiating factor distinguishing the saved from the lost is to be found in God. God's will and disposition is equivocal or two-sided. Pighius relates the saved and the lost, as those who accept and those who reject the offer of salvation, both to the same will of God. Calvin sees the saved and the lost as the elect and the reprobate, and each class is related to a different counsel or ordination within God.

This leads to the second aspect in which Pighius and Calvin differ. If the question of the relation of God to the saved and to the lost be raised, Pighius has a simple answer to give. God, he says, wills the salvation of men and for this purpose demands their conversion (§VIII.1). Where conversion takes place, salvation is enjoyed. Where it does not take place, not only is eternal life forfeit, but the single univocal will of God is set at nought. With this Calvin partly agrees and partly disagrees. It is true that God wills the salvation of men; it is further true that men are called to conversion; it is again true that where conversion takes place, there the blessings of salvation are enjoyed. But there is a difference also in what Calvin maintains. Conversion and its fruits are the work of the Spirit and therefore must be directly traced to God Himself. This is the question of order about which something has already been said. Election does not follow but precedes faith. Hence, while it is true that faith and salvation go together as Pighius says, faith is not the independent condition of salvation; for both faith and salvation are in fact consequent upon election (§VIII.2).

There thus appear two quite different ways of relating the saved and the lost to the will of God. Pighius relates them to an identical salvific will of God, the differential being found in men's different volition. Calvin relates them severally to a different determination by the will of God. A further difference is implied as a corollary. On Pighius' view, the reprobate are those who have by the exercise of their volition been able to thwart the general purpose of God for salvation. Their relation to the will of God is therefore negative, and only that of the elect is positive. For Calvin, however, the reprobate are, just as much as the elect, positively related to the will of God. For they carry out His counsel to destruction just as the elect carry out His counsel to salvation. Such unity as the will of God possesses must therefore be found at a more exalted level. It is in fact found by Calvin to reside in God's purpose for His own glory. This sublime purpose is equally served by salvation and by destruction, and the elect and the reprobate equally render Him honour. Only a very slight discrepancy between the two classes is allowed to appear at this point. The elect knowingly render God glory and thus directly forward His purpose, whereas the reprobate intend to withhold honour and reverence from Him, and yet, failing to accomplish their intention, they indirectly and despite themselves promote His glory and forward His purpose.

The defect involved in Pighius' account is indicated by Calvin (§VIII.2). It represents God and men as of equal status in such a way that each can oppose and thwart the other. Calvin puts this point positively. On such a view, he says, man has an independent contribution to make in the effecting of salvation. The operation of salvation is thus a work of co-operation between man and God. But the partition thereby implied is in fact most unequal. "What kind of a partition it would be, and how unequal, if God were responsible for our creation, while we were in this way responsible for our salvation —if God made us, but we saved ourselves." The more excellent work would then, Calvin says, be arrogated by man to himself. The point Calvin here makes is a valid one. It cannot seriously be maintained that God and man can be put, in the matter of salvation or any other matter, on an equal footing. It leads to man being required, as Calvin says, to do the "more excellent" part of the work. The objection may be stated more generally: it will not do to think of God and man as so related in their activity that the less God does the more man has to do, and *vice versa*. This will have to be referred to later.

But Calvin's representation involves a different but certainly not a lesser perplexity. The view he contradicts finds the differentia between the elect and the reprobate in the respective action of different men, and God is not directly involved in the discrimination. Calvin's view on the other hand traces the differentia back to God Himself, and different counsels, one for certain men to be saved and one that others be passed over and left to destruction, are found in God. The anxious question then arises whether the counsel to elect and the counsel to reprobate are related in an identical way to God or within God's purpose. Putting the thing in other words, do these two very different counsels equally represent and express the will of God and His intention towards men? It would be unfair to say that Calvin directly faces this question and gives an affirmative answer to it; but it is impossible to say that he provides the material for a denial. When he comes nearest to supplying an answer, it looks as though he regularly contented himself with a juxtaposition of the two counsels; and from this one can only conclude that he thinks of them as equal expressions of God's disposition towards men. He expressly rejects one solution which would allow for an imparity of relationship when he denies that we may distinguish between the sufficiency and the efficacy of Christ's work. We may not, he says (§IX.5), hold that "Christ suffered sufficiently for all, but efficaciously only for the elect". Further, he can say (§V.3): "to the gratuitous love with which the elect are embraced there corresponds on an equal and common level a just severity towards the reprobate". And referring to Augustine at another point (§VIII.2), he says that the salvation of the elect reposes in the faithful custody of God so that none perishes, and immediately continues to speak of the rest of mortal men, saying that they are not of this number, but rather are taken out of the common mass and made vessels of wrath, being born for the use of the elect. From such expressions, the conclusion must be drawn that Calvin regarded the relation of election and of reprobation as symmetrically related to the will of God, that election and reprobation are correlatives standing in an identical relation to God's will and equally expressing it. We are thus led to the forbidding doctrine of *predestinatio duplex*.

Only at a lower level does the respective relation of the elect and the reprobate to God manifest an imparity. Each class at least tends to display their status by characteristic fruit and signs, the reprobate by wickedness and the elect by the fruit of the Spirit. These characteristic types of conduct are differently related to God. Since men by themselves are quite incapable of doing or effecting anything good, what is good in or from them is attributable to God alone and to the operation of His grace upon them. The actions of the elect are therefore both proximately and remotely to be attributed to God. But in the case of the reprobate, another factor enters in to assume the role of proximate cause of the actions done, namely their own wicked volition, while to God is assigned only the remote cause of what they do. But this imparity remains upon the level of conduct only. Finally, it is annulled, in that both the elect and the reprobate are equally governed by divine decrees. Hence, this imparity is never built in to what Calvin has to say about Predestination as such. The symmetry of the relation existing between God and the elect and the reprobate respectively shows that Calvin does not take advantage of the perception which at other points on a lower level is clearly his.

Elsewhere (see *Commentaries*, Ezek 18.23, Jn 3.10, II Pet 3.9), the argument Calvin pursues brings him even closer to a realisation that some disparity exists between God and His different decrees of election and reprobation; but once again he turns aside from the insight without making full use of it. He suggests that, while the will of God is that all men should be saved, His *arcanum consilium* is that some be damned. "This will of God which He sets forth in His Word, does not prevent Him from decreeing what He would do with every individual." But in the end the distinction here made collapses: "Scripture does speak doubly of the will of God—because God has to transfigure Himself in order to condescend to us" (*Commentary*, I Tim 2.3-5). It is only we, because of our defective understanding who may speak of the will of God "in two sorts". His ultimate will has as object only His own glory, and this is equally served by election and by reprobation.

Is it possible to suggest a basis for the belief that the relation of the two to God and His will is not identical? How did it come about that Calvin failed to embody this element into his teaching? From where does the clue come to us that there is such an imparity, and where can we find a sound ground for supposing it? In some senses and to some extent, morality itself provides the clue and supplies the ground. A good case can be made out for holding that the nature of morality leads beyond the sphere in which it itself operates. Kant's way of putting this is, of course, that certain suppositions are necessary for the existence of morality, that those suppositions are not to be found here in the world of space and time, that without them morality is self-stultifying, and that they are consequently to be supposed fulfilled in the realm of the transcendental. A statement more agreeable to modern thought would be that good would not exist or would not be recognised and appreciated unless the universe did in fact and despite appearances accord it preferential treatment. It is this kind of preferential treatment which Calvin does not permit himself to suppose in God. This is a pity; and metaphysically it would be a fault.

But the basis of the imparity is primarily not anthropological or even moral, but theological; and it is from this point of view that the magnitude of Calvin's fault in failing to make place for it is revealed both in its essence and in its seriousness. As P. Maury says (*La Prédestination*, Labor et Fides, Geneva, 1957, p. 50), "in the Bible there is no kind of parallelism between negative election or rejection, and positive election or entry into grace". For Christian faith, God's preferential attitude to election over reprobation is revealed and validated in Jesus Christ. To this aspect we now turn.

4.3. The part of Christ in Predestination

The doctrine of Predestination must be thought out and stated christologically. What part does Calvin conceive of Christ as playing? Acts 2.23, Calvin points out (§V.1), declares that Christ was delivered to death by the determinate counsel and foreknowledge of God. Of course the death is carried out by the violence of men, but it was none the less ordained by the eternal decree of God. Christ was indeed driven to death, but it is not by chance or by merely human action. God deliberately decreed it. Thus in Peter's sermon, God's counsel is involved as well.

It follows that Christ is for us "the bright mirror of the eternal and hidden election of God" (§VIII.6). This and similar statements recur frequently. He is "the most excellent luminary of grace and Predestination" (§IV), for certainly the only begotten Son of God did not acquire this dignity by anything that He did or believed. It is by grace that He is such and so great as He is (loc. cit.). Predestination shines brightest in the Saint of saints. No more splendid mirror of Predestination exists than the Mediator Himself, who attained without merit such honour as to be the only begotten Son of God (§VIII.6).

Moreover, He is this for us. For, as Augustine says, He is the One destined to be our Head, and thus many are predestined to be His members (§IV). Hence, the term mirror does not represent all that is involved. Christ is also "earnest and pledge", for He came forth from the bosom of the Father to make us heirs of the heavenly kingdom by ingrafting us into His body (§VIII.4). Not only mirror, says Calvin, but also the earnest and pledge (§VIII.6).

Much the same thing is stated in other terms, when Calvin declares that Christ is a seal of our election. But at this point a further definition seems to be added (loc. cit.). "Christ is therefore said to manifest the name of the Father to us because by His Spirit He seals on our hearts the knowledge of our election testified to us by the voice of His Gospel." Thus Christ appears as the *ratio cognoscendi* of our election by God. "The certainty of our salvation is set forth to us in Christ" (loc. cit.). Or again, in greater detail, we have not to "toil to draw life out of the hidden recesses of God". For, as St Paul says, we were chosen in Christ before the foundation of the world. We have to begin with Christ in order to see that we are reckoned among God's peculiar people; and each may know himself to be an heir of the heavenly kingdom so long as he abides in Christ (loc. cit.). To the question how we know ourselves to be elect, Calvin returns the answer that "Christ is more than a thousand testimonies to me" (§VIII.7). And again (§VIII.4), Christ is the "manner in which God discharges His work of grace"; but why He takes the elect by the hand "has another superior cause, that eternal purpose, namely, by which He destined them to life".

This is indeed eloquent testimony to the place that Christ has in the election of men. But when all is said, it may still be asked whether it is enough. It is with moving words that Calvin enjoins the believer to know of his election and to enjoy all certainty and security by turning to Christ, Himself the first and most evidently elect man. For in Christ we have the revelation of God's eternal purpose of election. When Christ's place is thus defined, He is clearly the very instrument of God in our election. But this is not to secure for Christ a place in the framing of that divine purpose to election. If, as in the passage last quoted above, there is a real difference between the *manner* of our election which is Christ and the *cause* of our election which is the divine eternal purpose, then Christ after all is not the *fundamentum* of our election; He is not there as God frames His purpose to elect. (Cf. perhaps *Institutes*, 3.22.1: *gratiam istam Dei praecedit electio*.) Predestination is then *in Christo*, and *per Christum*, and in a sense also *propter Christum*. But for the primary ground of Predestination, we have to penetrate into the *divinae sapientiae adyta*, where we find it lodged in an *arcanum consilium*. And it appears that into these deep counsels, Christ has not been admitted. If this is true, we must beg leave to doubt whether Calvin really allowed to the fact that our election is in Christ its full significance and scope. This, as we shall see, is the fundamental reason why he can relate the elect and the reprobate identically to the will of God.

5. Concluding Comment
5.1. *Three inadequacies*

In the course of the critical comment, three points at which inadequacy of treatment showed itself in Calvin's presentation came to light. Since Predestination is a doctrine manifest in Scripture and indispensable to Christian faith, it is of importance that these inadequacies should be made good and the doctrine restated in a less vulnerable form. One concerned whether he had done enough to allay the complaint that his account of God's action fails to vindicate God's justice; the second concerned the parity of relation which his account seemed to establish between God and the two diverse decrees of election and reprobation; the third was christological and concerned the place accorded to Christ in the framing of the decrees. These three inadequacies are, however, not unrelated. It appears that if the third of them is corrected, modifications have to be carried out in the statement of the doctrine which constitute the correction of the other two.

The place of Jesus Christ can only be guaranteed by giving full weight to the significant statement of Eph 1.4, that God "hath chosen us in Jesus Christ before the foundation of the world". It is perhaps not necessary here to undertake the task of showing that this verse is no mere flash in the pan, that it is closely consonant with other Pauline passages, and that it accords with what in the main the Bible has to say about Predestination. Its significance can be briefly set forth in contrast to what Calvin has been seen to say. To accord to Christ an important place in the execution of the decrees falls short of what is demanded. Instrumentality is not a concept that adequately conveys the role that Christ must here be deemed to play. He must be regarded as not merely the agent but as the *fundamentum* of the decrees, so that they are framed not in His absence but really "in him". Where and when the counsels of God are determined, there and then Christ is present. The part which He plays in their execution is of course quite real and entirely indispensable; but it does not exhaust His role. He does not merely discharge counsels in which He has had no hand; their framing as well as their discharge is traceable to Him. This is only to take seriously the doctrine that God not only at and after but also before the incarnation is triune.

It follows from this that Calvin does not give good guidance when, to vindicate the justice of what God does in the execution of His decrees, he invokes the dark recesses, the *divinae sapientiae adyta*, as though there were, even after the revelation of Christ, a residuary darkness to which He is not Himself privy and for which He has no power of illumination. The unknowable that remains in God after His revelation in Christ is not an un-illumined area, but an unfathomable depth. The incarnation gives us the key to all God's nature, or it is not the complete revelation which Christianity has always considered it to be. Moreover, since the revelation takes the form of a real incarnation, the human attributes which Christ assumes are, in their measure, and so far as they go, adequate. Thus, for example, we may speak of God as love—not indeed that our love or any human love can fully comprehend the love of God, for that and how the infinite should become finite for our sakes is literally "unspeakable". Nevertheless, clothed as He was in flesh and manifesting in the flesh a love of such measure as led Him to make the supreme sacrifice, He gives His brethren the claim to possess a key to the divine love, which is in itself so much greater. With justice, as has already been said, the case is a little different. Of course the justice of God is the foundation of the moral order. In virtue of the incarnation,

we are entitled to take our understanding of justice as the key
to that order, and it is difficult to resist the conclusion that our
apprehension of justice is a more than usually reliable key to
justice wherever it occurs, even in the actions of God. The
foundation of the moral order and the key to it cannot contradict each other. But we are taught about justice also by the
coming of Christ. Here there opens out something which may
be called the "greater justice", since it goes beyond the
juridical and forensic justice with which we are familiar and
of which we have so ineradicable a sense. In the coming of
Christ is endorsed unmistakably what also appears in the rest
of the Bible: the justice of God is not confined to the execution
of justice, but includes also the promotion of justice. For these
purposes, justice may use two different instruments: by punishment, justice may be vindicated; but forgiveness may also be
used for its promotion. In Christ's work, we see both means of
justice in use. We may thus say that in Christ we know that
all God's works are just.

If this can in any sense claim to be a resolution of the difficulty regarding justice, it is not one of which Calvin can make
use. By his doctrine of the double decree, he is compelled to
relate both the elect and the reprobate to God in a similar
manner, and for vindication of the justice of this apparently
unjust procedure he has recourse to a hiddenness in God to
which men, even with the light of Christ's revelation, have no
access. Only by holding firmly to the entire adequacy of Christ's
revelation is another and less baffling solution to be found.

We are thus led to the other inadequacy whose presence has
been noted. Is Calvin right in holding a parity of relation
between God and the two decrees governing election and
reprobation? If Christ is given His rightful place in the determining of the counsels of God, it is impossible to maintain
a parity of relation. He came on His own testimony to "seek
and to save that which was lost"; and in the strictest sense we
may say that in His coming God pledges His preference for
one of the decrees over the other.

The sovereignty of God does not then consist in a magisterial
indifference which holds the two decrees in an equilibrium of
favour. It consists precisely in the fact that God exercises
sovereignty over both the classes indicated by the terms elect
and reprobate, and appropriately deals with them. There is

indeed a possibility of belief and a possibility of unbelief—an awful option which lies before every man. Indeed the coming of Christ precipitates this situation, for "if I had not come, they had not had sin". Under the sovereignty of God these options open out in all their significance, provoked, in a manner of speaking, by the coming of Christ. But as they equally open out at His coming, there appears also a distinction of treatment accorded to each. Unbelief is condemned at the cross—"why hast thou forsaken me?"; and belief is rewarded: "today shalt thou be with me in paradise". Christ is at the cross both the reprobate and the elect. He condemns the one state or condition in the cross, and He offers the other by the cross. The imparity of God's disposition to the two states thus becomes unmistakably clear, and no considerations of symmetry or of logical equality may be allowed to distort what the work of Christ has demonstrated. The cross takes place, and there election and reprobation are one. If this were all, if Good Friday were not succeeded by Easter Day, Calvin would have to be deemed right: election and reprobation equally subserve the glory of God and are equally related to His will. We should have to endorse the austere and sombre conclusions of *predestinatio duplex*. But in fact the resurrection takes place; and then only election survives the acid test, while reprobation is cancelled, literally crossed out.

5.2. Chosen in Christ before the foundation of the world

With a further comment based upon this text, this Introduction must come to an end. Christ must be allowed to occupy His rightful place where Predestination is being determined. He Himself is the elect and becomes the reprobate. But He is also "the firstfruits of many brethren". It is in this Christ that our Predestination takes place, and God predestines us as in Him. If this is so, it cannot be that we must opt one way or another, for belief or for unbelief, before our fate is determined. This determination certainly is not held up, impeded or delayed until we have exercised our choice. It has already been taken for us by God in Christ. If this is true, it further follows that in some sense the dice are loaded for us—God has pledged His preference in one direction rather than in another. He wills primarily to save and not to condemn, to elect and not to reprobate.

Yet this is not to be construed in such a sense that we must say that it is impossible for us to choose and to adhere to unbelief. We cannot even say that it is more difficult to do so than to choose and adhere to Christ. The imparity of God's disposition is not an immediate guarantee that we shall be saved; nor is it even an indication that we are more likely to be saved than lost. His preferential disposition to election leaves the two options still open before us. Issues of infinite moment depend upon whether we believe or not. These issues have not been foreclosed; they remain "live issues". What God's imparity of disposition, His predilection or preference for one option over against the other, does do is to write a different verdict upon each of them. We are predestined already in Christ. If by belief we adhere to Christ and so to this destiny, since He Himself enjoys eternal life (Rom 4.24) and righteousness (I Cor 5.18), we being in Him enjoy these also; and even the faith we have is *His* faith (see Karl Barth's interpretation of Gal 2.19 in *Evangelium und Gesetz*, Theologische Existenz Heute, no. 50, Chr Kaiser Verlag, München, 1956, p. 9f.). The other possibility is to contract out. It is equal in possibility with the first. But there is this salient difference, that over this possibility is the sign that crosses it out. The choice of this possibility is a cleaving to the No which God utters at the cross, instead of to the Yes of the resurrection which succeeds and supersedes the cross. As Karl Barth says, "the choice of the godless man is void" (*Church Dogmatics*, II, 2, T. & T. Clark, Edinburgh, 1957, p. 306).

Is such a choice ever made? can men "contract out"? does anyone choose to adhere to this No of God? We cannot of course answer this question with certainty. There is only One who discerns the hearts of men. But we must say that it is a possibility, and has all the reality of a possibility, and this makes it quite different from something which just is not. If finally this possibility is by any man's action given not only reality (for this it already has) but realisation, it is a strange and aberrant decision that is taken. It is and can be nothing else than the decision of evil for evil. This is where we can go no farther. For if evil were explicable, then it would be rational; and if it were rational, it would have parity of relation to God with the good. This would be once again to stand where Calvin's doctrine lands us, but not, I think, where Christians ought to stand.

Concerning the Eternal Predestination of God
by which He has chosen some men to salvation and left others to
their own destruction

and Concerning the Providence of God by which He governs
all human affairs

The Agreement of the Pastors of the Church
of Geneva

set forth by John Calvin

Geneva
at the office of John Crispin
1552

The translation is made from the Latin version in *Corpus Reformatorum* vol. XXXVI, John Calvin's Opera vol. VIII, Brunswick 1870, pp. 249-366.

The bracketed pagination in the Table of Contents is that of the *Corpus Reformatorum*.

The section numbers and headings have been inserted in the text to facilitate understanding and reference.

CONCERNING THE ETERNAL PREDESTINATION OF GOD

TABLE OF CONTENTS

THE pastors of the Church, to whom is entrusted the administration of the Word both in town and country, pray that God may grant to those most excellent men, their supreme lords, and to the Syndics and Senate of Geneva, a just and holy administration of the State and good success.

The same motive that impelled us to write this book, most excellent Sirs, constrained us also to dedicate it you, that it might go out under your name and auspices. The free election of God, by which He adopts for Himself whom He will out of the lost and damned generation of men, has hitherto been declared by us with reverence, sobriety, sincerity and frankness and has been peacefully received by the people. But now recently Satan, the father of all strifes, has introduced a widespread error, which attempts to destroy our doctrine which is drawn from the pure Word of God and to shake the faith of the whole people. But since this hungry hunter after vain-glory wishes to gain notoriety out of the very flame of the temple of God, lest he should gain the reward of his sacrilegious audacity for which he lies in wait, let his name remain buried in our silence. For the rest, since the harm he tried to do us was equally done to you, it is right that any fruit arising out of the matter should be applied to you also. And as we have found you vigorous and prudent judges in a worthy cause, we have thought it our duty for our part to testify our gratitude as we are able. The discharge of this duty will also clearly show what kind of doctrine it is that you have defended by your favour. For though it befits neither the noble rulers of the State nor the ministers of Christ to pay anxious heed to rumours, so that many perverse disparagements, which little by little collapse into the uproar they occasion, be despised by both with courage and dignity, yet it is of the greatest importance that the sum of the matter should remain in the hands of all and kept before their eyes, as though engraved on public notice-boards, to convict the false voices of the foolish, the vain or the wicked and at the same time to repress the frivolous whispers of the crowd. A rumour was spread around in many places that he was closely imprisoned, whereas he was free to fly about the city openly every day. You yourselves are the best witnesses with what malignity certain virulent people pretended that we demanded death as his punishment. Dignity and prudence can only refute such calumnies with contempt and quiet magnanimity, until they disappear. But on the other hand, it is both expedient and obligatory for us to set out the state of the case, lest the many unstable people, who must be reckoned with, should waver. Impiety creeps in like a cancer, as St Paul says, unless it be opposed. Now this defence, offered in your name to all the godly, will we hope be a strong and effectual remedy for healing those that are curable as well as a wholesome antidote for the healthy and sound. The subject is worthy of study by the sons of God, lest they neglect their heavenly origin and birth. For because the Gospel is called the power of God unto salvation to all who believe, some have made this a pretext for obliterating the election of God. But it ought to have occurred to them to ask whence faith arises. Scripture everywhere declares that God gives to His Son those who were His, calls those whom He elects, and begets again by His Spirit those He had adopted as sons; and finally that those men whom He teaches inwardly and to whom His arm is revealed believe. Hence, whoever holds faith to be earnest and pledge of grace confesses that it flows from divine election as its eternal source. Yet knowledge of salvation is not to be demanded by us out of the secret counsel of God. Life is set before us in Christ, who not only makes Himself known in the Gospel but also presents Himself to be enjoyed. Let the eye of faith look fixedly in this mirror, and not try to penetrate where access is not open. Since this is the way, let the sons of God walk in it, lest, by flying higher than is right, they plunge themselves into a deeper labyrinth than they had wished. For the rest, as there is no other gate into the kingdom of heaven than faith in Christ contained in the promises of the Gospel clearly set before us, it is the most crass stupidity not to acknowledge that the eyes of our mind are opened by God, since, before we were conceived in the womb, He chose us to be faithful. But it was the object of this impure and worthless fellow not only to destroy all knowledge of God's election from the mind of men, but also to overthrow His power completely. This is clear from those mad dreams of his which you have, written by his own hand, in your public records. There he affirms that faith does not depend on election, but rather that election rests upon faith; that none remain blind on account of innate corruption of nature, since all are really illumined by God; and that we do God injustice in saying that those whom He does not condescend to illumine by His Spirit are passed by. He affirms that all men in general and equally are drawn by God, and that distinction only begins with obstinacy; and that when God promises to make hearts of flesh out of hearts of stone, all that is meant is that we are to be capable of receiving the grace of God, this being promiscuously offered to the whole human race, though Scripture clearly declares it to be the singular privilege of the Church. As for the providence of God by which the world is ruled, the godly should confess and hold to this, that there is no reason why men should make God associate in their sins, or in any way involve Him with themselves as participant of the blame. Scripture teaches that the reprobate are also instruments of God's wrath, for by some He instructs His faithful in patience, and on others He inflicts the punishments which as enemies they merit. But this profane trifler contends that no act of God is just unless its plain reason lies before our eyes. Thus he removes the distinction between remote and proximate causes. He will not allow the sufferings imposed on the saintly Job to be considered the work of God, lest He should be made equally guilty with Satan and the Chaldaean and Sabaean robbers.

But we pass him by and come to grips with the other two, Albertus Pighius and Georgius the Sicilian. There is a double reason for this, as we shall explain. This ignorant pettifogger was able to offer nothing but what he drew from these two sources, thus making what was badly said worse. Dispute with him would accordingly have been profitless. To be content with one example: how Pighius and Georgius obscure the first chapter of Ephesians by their sophistries has been shown in its proper place. This was absurd enough. But still more disgraceful was this man's folly; for he did not blush to babble it all in your court and venerable assembly, and stubbornly to defend what he had babbled, maintaining that Paul in the passage is treating not of the common salvation of the godly but of his own and his colleagues' election to the apostolic office. To refute such a futile suggestion at once while[1] still fresh in memory was

---

[1] *extemplo*; Beza, Amst. and Niem: *exemplo*; French has: openly.

easy. If any attach themselves as disciples to such a master, they will certainly learn unfortunate theology, such as would deprive us all[1] of confidence in eternal life, since only the apostles would be partakers of divine election, reconciled to God through Christ and, blessed, or numbered in the society of the saints. The time to do all this was when the matter arose; it is not very appropriate to refute so foolish a fellow in a published book. We are indeed not unaware how much it would please him; nor would it be surprising to find so much audacity in one who throws off a monk's cowl and forthwith assumes the role of a physician. But to play the fool and nauseate many by gratifying him would be foreign to my usual moderation. Further, since those two are known and professed enemies of the Gospel, and one of them in attacking Calvin by name has declared war on us and on this Church, it seemed wiser to purge in printed books the poison of impious doctrine disseminated publicly, than by publishing dirges better left unsung to weary importunately the ears of men which have been already more than sufficiently vexed by superfluous contentions.

May the Lord God grant, noble and excellent Sirs, that, as you have hitherto done with the highest praise, you may continue by your faith and authority unwearyingly to defend to the very end the pure doctrine of the Gospel, which is everywhere so agitated by the hostile violence of the world; and that you may not cease to receive hospitably all the godly who flee to your protection; so that your city may be a safe sanctuary amid these horrid tumults and a faithful asylum for the members of Christ. So may it be that you find Him a perpetual protector of your salvation; for the dwelling-place that is dedicated to Him is safe by His power and will never fall.

1st January 1552

[1] *nos omnes*; ib: *non omnes.*

CONCERNING THE ETERNAL PREDESTINATION OF GOD

I. CALVIN'S OPPONENTS AND THEIR THESES

NINE[1] years have now elapsed since Albertus Pighius the Campanian, a man of clearly frenzied audacity, tried in the same book both to establish the freewill of man and to overthrow the secret counsel of God whereby He chooses some to salvation and destines others for eternal destruction. But because he attacked me by name, so as to stab at pious and sound doctrine through my side, it has become necessary for me to curb the sacrilegious fury of the man. However, I was at that time distracted by other business and was unable to embrace the discussion of both matters in a short space of time. But the first part being discharged, I undertook to write later, when

[1] In place of what is said here in pages 11-15 of the chief Latin edition, the French version presented to the magistracy has this briefer reading:

It seems to me that I have dealt adequately in the *Institutes* with what all Christians ought to think concerning this article of faith contained in Holy Scripture: to know, that is, that from among men God has chosen to salvation those whom He pleased, and has rejected the others, without our knowing why, except that its reason is hidden in His eternal counsel. But because Satan does not cease to raise up evil spirits to obscure, vex and even entirely overthrow this doctrine, in order that those who wish to adhere to the pure truth of God may be content with it, I much wanted to add this treatise to what I had already written before as more ample confirmation of what was there already said. In our time, there have been two principal enemies of God who have attacked this article of our faith, trying to abolish what Scripture shows us about predestination. I therefore address myself also to them and reply to all they produce to the contrary. For they have gathered all the trivialities which can shake or put doubts in unstable consciences, and all the blasphemies by which the wicked try to denigrate and defame the justice of God. The first of those I have mentioned is a Low German, Albert Pighius by name, a man of an impetuous and even furious spirit. The other has been a monk of St Benedict, called Georgius of Sicily, who alleged to foolish people that Jesus Christ had appeared to him and given him the understanding of all Scripture, and won much credence for a little time, so as to deceive and confuse an infinite number of people. All that they bring forward is so frivolous that it is almost superfluous for me to argue about it. Nevertheless, seeing the need, I did not wish to fail to discharge my office, to recover those not quite incurable as well as to offer a preservative to those who are not really sufficiently protected against the malice and devices of those gallants.

The sum of what has to be treated is what I have mentioned above, namely, that God of His pure and gratuitous goodness chooses from among men to call to salvation those whom it seems to Him good, and that the rest remain in their perdition. But before going further, it is well that readers be once more warned that this question is by no means a fickle subtlety, tormenting souls without fruit or purpose, but that it is a holy and useful disputation . . ., etc.

occasion served, about predestination. Shortly after my book on freewill appeared, Pighius died. So, not to insult a dead dog, I turned attention to other studies. And from that time on, I never lacked something to do. Further, as I had already fully dealt with this point of doctrine, expounding it clearly and proving it by the solid testimony of Scripture, this new labour did not seem so necessary that it could not be put aside. But today certain wofully idle spirits follow the example of Pighius and try to destroy all that Scripture maintains concerning the gratuitous election of the pious and the eternal judgment of the reprobate. So I have considered it my duty to collect and briefly refute these frivolous objections by which they delude both themselves and others, lest the contagion spread farther. Among these others there emerged in Italy a certain Georgius, a Sicilian, an ignorant man, worthy rather of contempt than of censure, except that a reputation gained by fraud and imposture gives him great power for harm. For when a Benedictine monk, he remained hid in his cell; until Lucius Abbas, one of the Tridentine fathers, raised him into eminence by false commendation, hoping from his shoulders himself to take flight into heaven itself. This worthless fellow mendaciously stated that Christ had appeared to him and appointed him interpreter of all Scripture; and without much difficulty he persuaded many to believe as true what he himself with a folly, stupid and shameless and worse than vain, alleged. And, to pursue his story to the last act, he trumpeted forth his crazy visions with such confidence, that he made his inexperienced adherents, already bound by prejudice, quite astonished. And certainly the greater part of men today are worthy of such prophets; for partly their heart is obstinate in wickedness and accepts no remedy, and partly their ears itch with insatiable desire for depraved speculations. There are perhaps others who might be mentioned more gladly or honourably. But I suppress their names, for I wish my readers to understand how frivolous and worthless are all their objections.

In Pighius and Georgius the Sicilian I see the equals and close counterparts of monsters. For though I confess that they differ in some respects, yet in contriving enormities of error, in licence of revelling, in impious and audacious adulteration of Scripture, in proud contempt of truth, in egregious impudence, and in violent loquacity, there is found the closest resemblance and equality. There is only this difference, that Pighius inflates the muddy bombast of his magniloquence and carries himself with the greater pomp and ostentation; while the other borrows the boots of his exaltation from his alleged revelation. And while both agree in attempting to overthrow predestination, they differ later in the fictions they propose. Both imagine that it lies within his freedom whether one is partaker of the grace of adoption; and it does not depend on the counsel of God who are elect and who reprobate; but that each determines for himself one state or the other by his own will. That some believe in the gospel and others remain unbelieving is a difference, they hold, arising not from God's free election or His secret counsel, but from the will of each individual.

For the rest, Pighius expounds his opinion thus. God created all men to salvation by an immutable counsel and without distinction. But as He foresaw the defection of Adam, in order that His election might nevertheless remain firm and stable, He applied a remedy which should be common to all. So the election of the whole human race is made stable in Christ, so that no one may perish except the man who deletes his name from the book of life by his obstinacy. On the other hand, as God foresaw that some would persist to the last in malice and contempt of grace, these He reprobated by His foreknowledge, unless they should repent. This is the source of reprobation, and the wicked deprive themselves of the universal benefit of election outside the counsel and will of God. He declares that all who teach that certain men are positively and absolutely chosen to salvation and others destined to destruction, think of God unworthily, attributing to Him a severity alien to His justice and goodness. Here he explicitly condemns the opinion of Augustine.[1] To show that the foreknowledge of God detracts in no way from our freedom of will, he resorts to that subtlety of Nicolas of Cusa: God did not foresee as future the things that were known to Him from eternity but regarded them in their present aspect. Yet in his customary manner, this imposter prides himself as if he were proffering some recondite something or other never heard before straight from the tripod of Apollo, whereas it is the trite prattle of a schoolboy. But since he still feels himself held and impeded, he introduces a double foreknowledge of God:[2] God took the decision of creating man to

---

[1] Bk. 8, ch. 1.   [2] Bk. 8, ch. 2.

live before He foreknew the fall; so that the thought of man's salvation took precedence of the foreknowledge of his death in the mind of God Himself. When he has rolled out these things in a muddy torrent of words, he thinks he has so overwhelmed the sense of his readers that discrimination is at an end; but I hope by my brevity presently to dispel the darkness of his loquacity. Georgius invents the suggestion that neither this man nor that is predestined to salvation, but that God has appointed a time in which He will save the whole world. To this end, he distorts certain passages from Paul: the mystery which had been hid from ages and generations is now made manifest by the advent of Christ and the preaching of the Gospel (Rom 16.25; Eph 3.9; Col 1.26). So he slips away in fancied safety, as if there were no plain scriptural testimony that some are chosen by God to salvation and others are passed by. In short, he considers no time but that of the New Testament.

II. CALVIN'S CONTRARY THESIS

The *Institutes* testify fully and abundantly to what I think, even should I add nothing besides. First of all, I beg my readers to recall the admonition made there. This matter is not a subtle and obscure speculation, as they falsely think, which wearies the mind without profit. It is rather a solid argument excellently fitted to the use of the godly. For it builds up faith soundly,[1] trains us to humility, elevates us to admiration of the immense goodness of God towards us, and excites us to praise this goodness. There is no consideration more apt for the building up of faith than that we should listen to this election which the Spirit of God testifies in our hearts to stand in the eternal and inflexible goodwill of God, invulnerable to all storms of the world, all assaults of Satan and all vacillation of the flesh. For then indeed our salvation is assured to us, since we find its cause in the breast of God.[2] For thus we lay hold of life in Christ made manifest to faith, so that, led by the same faith, we can penetrate farther to see from what source this life proceeds. Confidence of salvation is founded upon Christ and rests on the promises of the gospel. Nor is it a negligible support when, believing in Christ, we hear that this is divinely given to

---

[1] From this point onwards, the French version follows the Latin closely.

[2] French version has: in His will which never alters.

us, that before the beginning of the world we were both
ordained to faith and also elected to the inheritance of heavenly
life. Hence arises an impregnable security.[1] The Father who
gave us to the Son as His peculiar possession is stronger than
all, and will not suffer us to be plucked out of His hand. Here
then is no commonplace cause for humility, as a man discerns
so different a condition in those who have a common nature.
Wherever the sons of God turn their eyes, they light upon
remarkable examples of blindness and stupidity which horrify
them. Knowing themselves to be illumined in the midst of this
darkness, they ask how it happens that others in the midst of
clear light remain blind.[2] Experience convinces them that,
though once the eyes of their mind were closed, now they are
open[3]—who thus differentiates them? For this is certain, that
those who voluntarily remain ignorant of the difference
between them and others have not yet learned to render to God
what is His own. No one doubts that the root of piety and the
mother of all virtues is humility. But how is he to be humble
who will not hear of the original misery from which he has been
delivered, and who, by extending the beneficence of God
promiscuously to all, does all in his power to diminish it?
Certainly they are far from honouring the grace of God as it
merits, who declare that, while it is common to all, it effectually
resides in them because they have embraced it by faith. For all
the time they would keep the cause of faith out of sight, namely
that, elected to be sons by grace, they have afterwards bestowed upon them the spirit of adoption. What kind of gratitude
is it if, endowed with an incomparable benefit, I only profess
myself debtor on equal terms with him who has received hardly
a hundredth part of it? Hence, if to honour the goodness of
God it is chiefly necessary to remember how much we are
indebted to Him, they are malicious injurers of God who consider the doctrine of eternal election burdensome and vexatious.
For if it is buried out of sight,[4] half the grace of God must
vanish with it. Let them clamour who will[5]—we shall always
equip the doctrine of gratuitous election as we teach it with

1 French version adds: as our Lord Jesus Himself says.

2 French adds: unless there be a gift not indifferently bestowed upon all.

3 French has: how has God opened their eyes, although they once had them
closed just like those who remain unbelieving?

4 French has: if it is trampled out of sight.

5 French has: Let the malicious and those of depraved judgment murmur.

this maxim, for without it the faithful cannot adequately apprehend how great is the goodness of God by which they are effectually called to salvation. I touch lightly on these things which in their own place will be dealt with in a more adequate manner, lest anyone, avoiding a thing which it is supremely needful to know, should later feel gravely injured by its neglect. If we are not ashamed of the gospel, we must confess what is there plainly declared. God, by His eternal goodwill, which has no cause outside itself, destined those whom He pleased to salvation, rejecting the rest; those whom He dignified by gratuitous adoption He illumined by His Spirit, so that they receive the life offered in Christ, while others voluntarily disbelieve, so that they remain in darkness destitute of the light of faith.

III. SUPPORTING EVIDENCE FROM ST PAUL

Against this judgment of God, many dogs petulantly rise up.[1] Indeed some of them do not hesitate to attack God openly, asking why God, foreseeing the future ruin of Adam, did not order human affairs better. For restraining such people, there is no better means than Paul shows us. This question was raised: How can God be just in showing mercy upon whom He will and in hardening whom He will? Such human audacity he deems unworthy of reply, except to remind them of their rank and status: O man, who art thou that repliest against God? (Rom 9.20). Profane men[2] babble about his concealing the absurdity of the thing with silence for want of an answer; but the matter is quite otherwise. For the apostle adopts an axiom not only accepted by pious minds, but engraved on common sense: the inscrutable judgment of God is greater than men can penetrate. And who, I ask, would not be ashamed to comprehend within the measure of his mind all the causes of the works of God? For the question hinges upon this, whether there is no justice of God except what we can conceive. To formulate this in a word: is it lawful to measure the power of God by our natural sense? There is no one who would not immediately reply that all the senses of men concentrated in one man must succumb before the immense power of God. Yet as soon as a specific reason is not apparent

---

[1] French has: who fret against this admirable counsel of God.

[2] French has: certain wags.

in the works of God, somehow or other they are prepared to appoint a day[1] for judging Him. What therefore could be more opportune and apt than this admonition of Paul: those who elevate themselves above the heavens entirely forget what they are. Suppose God to cede His rights and offer Himself ready to render a reason. When it came to those secret counsels which the angels adore with trembling, who would not be stunned and amazed before such glory? How remarkable is the madness of men who are more audacious to subject God to themselves than to dare to stand on equal ground with some pagan judge![2] You find it grievous and hateful that God's power and deeds are greater than your mind conceives; yet to an equal of yours you will concede the right of enjoying his own judgment. Do you dare to mention the name of God while in so furious a frame of mind?[3] What does God's name mean to you? Will you assert that Paul is destitute of reason,[4] because he does not drag God from His throne and set Him before you for cross-examination? We on our side are assured that the holy apostle in the first place restrains with fitting gravity the wild madness of those who do not shrink from impugning the justice of God; and that secondly he gives to the worshippers of God a more useful counsel than if he had exalted them on eagles' wings above the clouds. For more excellent than wisdom is the soberness of mind which is regulated by the fear of God and keeps within the limits of intelligence prescribed by Him. Let proud men defame this sobriety, calling it by the name of ignorance, if they will; but let it hold fast the height of true wisdom,[5] that, believing the will of God to be the supreme justice, it ascribe to Him His proper glory.

But this does not satisfy Pighius and his fellows. For, pretending a concern for the honour of God, they bark at us as if we were imputing to Him a cruelty quite alien to His nature. He denies that there is any dispute between him and God. What or whose cause then is it that Paul upholds? After laying down this axiom, that God hardens whom He will and has mercy on whom He will, he supposes the retort:[6] Why does He still find fault? who resists His will? To such blasphemy he

---

[1] French has: to summon Him.   [2] French has: some village judge.
[3] French has: while they babble of God and religion.
[4] French has: that St Paul is at the bottom of his form.
[5] French has: wisdom now.
[6] French has: in the person of the slanderers, he retorts with the demand.

opposes simply the power of God. If those who attribute the hardening of men to His eternal counsel invest God with the character of tyrant, we are certainly not the author of this opinion.[1] If those who think His will to be stronger than all other causes do God injury, Paul taught this before us. Let them dispute with him. For in the present matter we contend for nothing which is not taught by him. Yet about these dogs I would not be over anxious. I am moved rather by anxiety for some otherwise decent men who, fearing to ascribe to God anything unworthy of His goodness, are terrified at what God says of Himself by the mouth of Paul. My express concern is the godly one of clearing God's justice from all calumny. Such modesty would even be worthy of praise, were it not the product of peevishness inflated by a certain secret arrogance; for such men speak out of their own natural sense.[2] For why should they fear to concede anything to the power of God beyond the grasp of their own mind lest His justice be imperilled, except for the reason that they do not hesitate to subject the tribunal of God to their own understanding? Paul shows how intolerable is the pride of the man who assumes to himself the judgment of his brother, since there is one judge by whom we all stand or fall, and to whom every knee must bow (Rom 14.10). What madness therefore for man to raise his hackles against this judge Himself by measuring His power by natural sense! Those therefore who plead that modesty like this prevents them endorsing Paul's doctrine must first confess that the praise they accord to God's justice is restricted to their own mind and sense; and then too, if in reality agreeing with us, they prefer none the less to suppress this doctrine for fear of giving free rein to the impudence of the wicked, the precaution is quite preposterous. As if the honour of God were to be protected by our lies! Not only does God Himself not delegate such patronage to us,[3] but in the book of Job pronounces it hateful to Him. Let such people therefore take care lest, by affecting a greater prudence than the Lord prescribes in His Word, they make themselves guilty of a double folly.

The moderation they commend is most useful for repressing the blasphemies of the wicked. But if they think thus easily to

---

[1] French has: but the Holy Spirit.

[2] This last phrase wanting in French version.

[3] French has: He frees us from commending Him by such means.

put the bridle upon such rebels against God by their words, their confidence is ridiculous. When Paul has discussed the hidden counsels of God so far as is needful, he as it were puts out his hand to forbid further advance. Restless spirits will kick and rear and leap over the limit set them with acrobatic facility.[1] How then will they subside at the nod of this or that trainer who encloses their course with narrower fences?[2] As well think to hold with a cobweb a horse prancing fiercely over the fencing it has broken.[3] But, you say, in a matter so hard and obscure, nothing is better than to think soberly. Who denies it? But at the same time it must be observed what the best kind of sobriety is, lest we suffer what has befallen the papists, who, to hold their adherents in obedience,[4] make them like brute beasts. Is this Christian simplicity, to fly from the knowledge of the things God shows as if it were harmful? Here, they say, we may be ignorant without detriment. As if the heavenly teacher were not the best judge of what and how much we should know! Therefore, lest we should be tossed by the waves, or blown about in mid-air in doubt and uncertainty, or put our foot in too deep and be drowned in the abyss, let us allow ourselves to be ruled and taught of God, contented by His simple Word and wanting to know nothing more than is to be found there, even if the faculty were given us. This docility, by which a pious man keeps all his natural senses under the Word of God, is the true and only rule of wisdom. For it is safe to follow, however far He who is the way with outstretched hand leads us, whose Spirit also spoke through apostles and prophets; and to be ignorant of those things which are not taught in the school of God far excels all the insight of the human mind. Therefore, Christ enjoins His sheep both to listen to His voice and to stop their ears to the voice of strangers. Indeed it cannot be otherwise than that vain winds of error blow from every quarter through the soul that is devoid of sound doctrine. Further, I can declare with all truth that I should never have spoken on this subject, unless the Word of God had led the way, as indeed all godly readers

[1] French adds: not observing the prohibition of the Holy Spirit.

[2] French has: Now if any people retract from what St Paul said, wishing to observe limits stricter than Scripture sets, I pray you, do those who are so fickle remain quietly within their appetite?

[3] French has: having burst bridle, halter and bar.

[4] French has: who do not allow for true simplicity.

of my earlier writings, and especially of my *Institutes*, will readily gather. But this present refutation of the enemies who oppose me will throw some fresh light.

IV. SUPPORTING EVIDENCE FROM ST AUGUSTINE

But since the authority of the ancient Church is offensively brought against me, it is perhaps worth while to say at the outset how unjustly the truth of Christ is smothered by this enmity, partly in error and partly in frivolity. But I would rather disperse this accusation, such as it is, with the words of Augustine than with my own.[1] For the Pelagians at one time vexed this holy man with the same reproach, that he had against him all other writers of the Church. He replies first that, before the rise of Pelagius' heresy, the fathers did not teach so precisely and exactly about predestination; and this is a fact. What need is there therefore, he says, to scrutinise the works of those writers who, before the heresy arose, thought it unnecessary to devote themselves to this difficult question?; but this, I do not doubt, they would have done, if enemies of predestination had compelled them to do so. This reply is both wise and ingenious. For unless the enemies of the grace of God had not worried him, he would never have so devoted himself to discussion of God's election, as he says himself. For in the work which he entitles *Concerning the Gift of Perseverance*,[2] he says: This predestination of the saints is certain and manifest; but necessity later compelled me to defend it more diligently and laboriously, when discussing it against a new sect. For we have learned that each heresy introduces into the Church its own particular question; and Holy Scripture has to be defended more diligently against these, than if no such need compelled it. For what was it that compelled us in that work more fully and simply to defend the passages of Scripture in which predestination is set forth? It was what the Pelagians say, that the grace of God is given according to merit—which is nothing but the negation of grace. Moreover, a little earlier[3] he had denied that prejudice should attach to his books on the score of their lack of antiquity. I think no one, he says, can be so unjust and envious as to forbid me to contribute to this subject. But afterwards he also contends that from the testimony of

---

[1] *De Praedest. Sanct.*, cap. 14.

[2] Cap. 20 [cited here and elsewhere in *C.R.* as *De Bono Perseverantiae*].   [3] Cap. 12.

certain fathers it could be gathered that they did not think differently from what he presently taught. Not to mention others, most obvious is the citation from Ambrose:[1] Whom Christ has mercy on, He calls. And again, if He had so willed, He would have made devoted men out of careless; but God calls whom He condescends to call, and makes religious whom He will. Who does not see that the entire sum of the question is comprised in these few words? A reason is assigned why all do not come to Christ to obtain salvation: that God does not effectually touch their hearts. He declares that the conversion of a man proceeds out of the gratuitous election of God; nor does he hide the fact that the reason why some are called and some are reprobated lies solely within His will. No one endowed with even mediocre judgment can fail to see that in these three summaries the state of the whole question is comprised and defined. Further, Augustine is so much at one with me that, if I wished to write a confession of my faith, it would abundantly satisfy me to quote wholesale from his writings. But, not to be too prolix on the present occasion, I shall be content with three or four passages by which it will be established that not even in a single point does he differ from me. From the whole course of the work, it could be established even more fully how solidly he agrees with me in every particular. In his work *Concerning the Predestination of the Saints*, he says[2] he contends against those who deny that the human race is born guilty of the sin of Adam, that the wills of men are prevented by the grace of God, and that no one is capable of beginning or completing any good work by himself. But what he rather wishes to do appears as the argument itself proceeds. For he goes on:[3] Lest anyone should say, my faith, my righteousness, or something of the kind, distinguishes me from others, the great teacher of the Gentiles meets all such thoughts by saying: What hast thou that hast not received? (I Cor 4.7)—from whom, unless from Him who distinguishes you from others in not giving to them what He gave to you? He goes on:[4] Faith therefore from beginning to end is the gift of God; and that this gift is given to some and not to others, no one can at all doubt, unless he wish to contest the most manifest testimonies of Scripture. But why it is not given to all ought not to disturb the believer, for he believes that all came under most just

[1] Cap. 19.   [2] Cap. 1.   [3] Cap. 5.   [4] Cap. 9.

condemnation by the sin of one; and why God delivers one man and not another are matters constituting His inscrutable judgments and His uninvestigable ways. Again,[1] if it be examined and enquired how anyone is worthy, there are some who will say: By their human will. But we say: By grace or divine predestination. Later he adds:[2] The Saviour and Son of God Himself is the most excellent luminary[3] of grace and predestination. For answer this: How did that Man merit being taken up by the Word into unity of person with the co-eternal Father so as to be the only begotten Son of God?[4] What good work preceded in such a case as this? what prior good did He do? what believe? what prayer offer, that He should come to such dignity? Here someone or other may murmur against God, saying: Why should it not have been me? Suppose the answer be given: O man, who art thou that repliest against God? Suppose that this does not restrain him and that his impudence increases and he says: What is this I hear, Who art thou, O man? since I am a man as He is of whom you speak, why am I not what He is? For by grace He is such and so great as He is. Why is grace different when the nature is the same? For certainly there is no acceptance of persons with God. What, I will not say Christian,[5] but madman would speak thus? Therefore, let our head appear as the origin of grace, which flows hence through all members, according to the measure of each. This is the predestination of the saints, which shines brightest in the Saint of saints. And a little later:[6] As He is the One predestined to be our head, so many of us are predestined to be His members. And lest anyone should attribute it to faith that one is preferred to another, Augustine denies that those who believe are chosen; rather they are chosen in order to believe. Similarly in the Epistle to Syxtus:[7] Why does this man believe and that not? why does God deliver this man rather than that?—let him who can, search so great an abyss; but let him beware of the precipice. Again in another place:[8] Who created the reprobate but God? And why,

---

[1] Cap. 10.   [2] Cap. 15.   [3] French has: mirror.

[4] French has: did He merit that this human nature which He took should be united in the same person to the eternal wisdom of God, etc.

[5] French has: miscreant.   [6] Cap. 17.

[7] Ep. 105 (Migne 194); Beza and Amst. have: Sextus; the French version: Sixt.

[8] Epistle to Boniface, 106 (Migne 186) [the letter seems, however, to be by Alypius and Augustine to Paulinus].

unless He willed it? Why did He will it?—O man, who art thou that repliest against God? And again elsewhere,[1] after proving that God is moved by no human merit, in making them obedient to His commands, but renders them good for evil, for His own sake and not for theirs, he then adds: If any should ask why God should make some His sheep and not others, the apostle, fearing this question, exclaims: O the depth, etc. (Rom 11.33). Just as Augustine derives the beginning of election from the gratuitous volition of God, and grounds reprobation in His mere will, so he teaches that the security of our salvation is also grounded nowhere else. For, writing to Paulinus,[2] he affirms that those who do not persevere do not belong to the calling of God which is efficacious and without repentance. But why some persevere and others do not is a matter hidden but not unjust. For this belongs to the depth of His judgments, which are called judgments precisely lest we imagine them unjust. More fully in another work, he contends that perseverance is bestowed upon the elect and from it they can never fall away.[3] Why He should not give perseverance to those to whom He gives an inclination[4] to live in a Christian manner, I confess myself ignorant. For not in arrogance but in recognition of my limitations, I hear Paul saying: O man, who art thou? Again, when Christ asked that the faith of Peter should not fail, what else did He ask but that he should have a most free, strong, invincible and persevering determination in faith? Then he added: It is wonderful, very wonderful, that to certain sons of His, whom He regenerated in Christ and to whom He gave faith, hope and love, He should not also give perseverance, when He remits the misdeeds of other stranger sons and makes them His. Who will not marvel at this? who will not be greatly surprised? Certainly here the judgments of God, since they are just and profound, are not to be censured or penetrated. Among them is also that which we are discussing, concerning perseverance.[5] Of both therefore, we exclaim: O the depth! But earlier, he had said:[6] The foundation of God standeth sure, having this seal, The Lord

---

[1] *Ad Bonif.*, lib. 4, cap. 6.   [2] *Ep.* 59 (Migne 149).
[3] *De Corrept. et Grat. ad Valent.*, cap. 8.
[4] French has: some good inclination (the rest omitted).
[5] This phrase is wanting in the French version.
[6] Cap. 7 of the same book.

knows them that are his (II Tim 2.19). The faith of these, which works by love, either does not fail at all, or, if there be any in whom it does fail, it is restored before this life is ended; the iniquity which interrupted it is removed, and their perseverance is reckoned up to the end. But those who are not destined to persevere and thus fall away from Christian faith, so that the end of life finds them in this state, are without doubt not reckoned in that number, even at the time when they lived well and piously. For they were not separated by the foreknowledge of God and predestination from the mass of perdition, and therefore were not called according to the purpose. But lest anyone be disturbed[1] because those sometimes fall away who had been thought the sons of God, he meets the perplexity thus:[2] Let no one think that those fall away who were of the predestined, called according to the purpose and truly sons of the promise. For those who appear to live piously may be called sons of God; but since they will eventually live impiously and die in that impiety, God does not call them sons in His foreknowledge. There are sons of God who do not yet appear so to us, but now do so to God; and there are those who, on account of some arrogated or temporal grace, are called so by us, but are not so to God. Those who are ordained to life are understood to be given to Christ. These are predestined and called according to the purpose, of whom none perishes; and on this account, no one, though he change from good to bad, ends his life so. For he is ordained and hence given to Christ that he should not perish but have eternal life. A little later Augustine says: Those who by the most provident disposition of God are foreknown, predestined, called, justified and glorified, are the sons of God, not only before they were regenerated, but before they were born at all, and they are quite unable to perish.[3] Then he assigns the reason: Because God works all things together for good to such as these, and this to such a degree that, if any of them deviate or wander, He makes even this turn to their advantage, for they return to Him more humble and experienced than before. If the thing be taken to a higher level and the question be raised about the

---

[1] *perturbet* in all Latin versions, but *perturbetur* is certainly to be read (French: that no one be troubled).

[2] Cap. 9.

[3] Almost all that is here taken from Augustine is expressed more briefly and shortly in the French version.

creation of man, Augustine meets it thus:[1] We make most sound confession of what we most rightly believe, that God the Lord of all things, who made all things very good, foreknew that evil would arise out of this good, and also knew that it contributed more to His glory to bring good out of evil than not to allow evil at all; so He ordained the life of men and angels so that in it He might first show what freewill could do, and then what the gift of His grace and the judgment of His justice could do. In his Manual to Laurentius[2] he at greater length settles all residual doubt. When in the last day, he says, Christ shall appear to judge the world, then what the faith of the pious now holds fast before it is manifest to their comprehension, will appear in the clearest light of knowledge—how sure, immutable and efficacious is the will of God; how many things He can do but does not will to do, while willing nothing that He cannot do; and how true is what the Psalmist sings in Ps 115.3: Our God hath done whatsoever He hath pleased. This would certainly not be true if He willed some things and did not do them. Nothing therefore is done unless He omnipotently willed it should be done, either by permitting it to be done or by doing it Himself. Nor may it be doubted that God did well in permitting to be done all that is ill done. For this is not permitted except by righteous judgment. Hence, though the things that are evil, in so far as they are evil, are not good, yet it is good that there be not only good but also evil things. For unless there were this good, that evil things existed, they would by no means be permitted to exist by omnipotent goodness. For without doubt it is as easy for Him to do what He wills as to permit what He does not will. Unless we believe this, we imperil the beginning of our faith, by which we confess belief in God almighty. Augustine then adds this conclusion:[3] These are the mighty works of God, excellent in all His acts of will, and so excellent in wisdom that when angelic and human creation had sinned, that is had done not what He willed but what it willed, God, through the same creaturely will which did what the creator did not will, nevertheless fulfilled what He willed, Himself superlatively good using for good even evil things to the damnation of those whom He had justly predestined to punishment and to the salvation of those whom He had mercifully predestined to grace. For so far as they were

---

[1] *De Corrept. et Grat.*, cap. 10. [2] Cap. 95 seq. [3] Ibid., cap. 100.

concerned, they did what was contrary to God's will; but as far as the omnipotence of God is concerned, they did not succeed in effecting it. In their very acting against the will of God, the will of God concerning them was none the less done. Mighty therefore, are the works of God and excellent in all His acts of will, so that in a marvellous and ineffable way that cannot be done without His will which is yet done contrary to His will. For it would not be done if He did not permit it, and permission is given not without but by His will. These few references are extracted out of many, so that the reader may clearly see[1] what modesty Pighius has in opposing Augustine to us so as to claim him as ally in his errors. As the discussion continues, further use will be made of the testimony of this holy man.

V. The Witness of Scripture

V.1. St Paul and St Peter

We turn now to what is the primary concern, to show that nothing is taught by me concerning this matter that is not plainly declared by God to us all in the sacred scriptures. This is that the salvation of the faithful depends upon the eternal election of God, and that for this no cause can be given except His gratuitous good pleasure. Paul's words in the first chapter of Ephesians are clear (v. 3): Blessed be God who hath blessed us in Christ, according as He hath chosen us before the foundation of the world. Now I hear Pighius[2] babble something: The whole human race is chosen in Christ, so that whoever should lay hold of Him by faith may obtain salvation. But in this invention there are two gross errors which can be instantly refuted by the words of Paul.

For first there is certainly a mutual relation between the elect and the reprobate, so that the election spoken of here cannot stand, unless we confess that God separated out from others certain men as seemed good to Him.[3] It is this that is expressed by the word predestinating, afterwards twice repeated. Further he calls those chosen who are by faith engrafted

[1] French has: as a preparatory lesson, so that they do not reject as novel what they will see to have been so well expressed by this sacred doctor, and also that they may recognise how closely I am in accord with him (the rest omitted).

[2] French has: and those like him.

[3] French has: for God in choosing has separated His own from among others, so that He cannot elect without electing some and rejecting others.

into the body of Christ; and that this is something not common to all men is plain. Paul therefore refers to those only whom Christ condescends to call after they have been given to Him by the Father. To make faith the cause of election is quite absurd and at variance with the words of Paul. For, as Augustine wisely observes,[1] he does not call them elect because they are about to believe, but in order that they may believe; he does not call them elect whom God foresaw would be holy and immaculate, but in order that they might be made so. Again, God did not choose us because we believed, but in order that we might believe, lest we should seem first to have chosen Him. Paul emphasises that our beginning to be holy is the fruit and effect of election. Hence, they act most preposterously who place election after faith.[2] Then, when Paul lays down as the unique cause of election the good pleasure of God which He has in Himself, he excludes all other causes. Therefore Augustine rightly enjoins us to return to this point, lest we should boast of the good pleasure of our own will. Paul continues (Eph 1.8): God abounded towards us in all prudence, having made known to us the mystery of His will, according to His good pleasure which He purposed in Himself. Thus, we are told, the grace of illumination, like a river, flows from the fountain of that eternal counsel which had before been hidden. This is far removed from the thought that God in choosing us had any regard to faith; for faith could not have existed, unless God had appointed it for us by the grace of His adoption. Paul further confirms this, declaring that God was moved by no external cause; He Himself and in Himself was author and cause of our being elected while yet we were not created, and of His afterwards conferring faith upon us. As Paul says (v. 11): According to His purpose who effects all things according to the counsel of His will. Who does not see that the eternal purpose of God is set over against ours? Augustine, too, pondered this passage deeply. He interprets: God so works out all things as to effect in us the very will by which we believe. It is now, I think, sufficiently demonstrated who they are whom God calls by the Gospel to the hope of salvation, whom He engrafts into the body of Christ, and whom He makes heirs of eternal life: it is those whom by His eternal and secret

[2] *De Praedest. Sanct.*, cap. 17, 18, 19.
[2] French has: as if the root should be placed after the fruit.

counsel He adopted to Himself as sons. So far was God from being moved by their faith to adopt them, that rather election is the cause and beginning of faith. Hence election is in order before faith.

Equally plain is what we have in the eighth chapter of Romans. For after saying that all things are an assistance to the faithful who love God, lest men should seek the source of their happiness in themselves, as if by their love they anticipated God and merited such benefit from Him, Paul immediately adds by way of correction: Who are called according to His purpose. Thus we see that he expressly secures priority for God; for by His calling He causes them to begin to love Him who could do nothing but hate. For, examine the whole race of man, and what propensity for loving God will be found there? Why, Paul in the same chapter declares all the senses of the flesh to be at enmity to God. If all men are by nature enemies and adversaries of God, it is plain that by His calling alone are those separated out who put hatred aside and turn to love Him. Further, there can be no doubt that it is that efficacious calling that is here denoted, by which God regenerates those whom He has first adopted to Himself as sons. For Paul does not say simply *called*. This commonly is applicable to the reprobate whom God promiscuously invites to penitence and faith along with His own sons. What he says is *called according to His purpose*; and this purpose must be stable in itself and certain in its effect. To expound this passage as referring to man's purpose is, as Augustine admirably argues,[1] absurd. The context itself removes every scruple, so that the need of any other interpreter is obviated. For there is added: Whom He predestinated or appointed, them He also called; and whom He called, them He also justified. Here clearly the apostle speaks of a certain number whom God destined as a property peculiar to Himself. For though God calls very many by other means, and especially by the external ministry of men, yet He justifies and finally glorifies none except those He ordains to life. The calling is therefore a certain and specific calling, which seals and ratifies the eternal election of God so as to make manifest what was before hidden in God.

I know the objections which many make here: when Paul says that those are predestinated whom God foreknew, he

---

[1] *Ad Bonif.*, lib. 2, cap. 9, *et aliis locis.*

means that each is elected in view of his faith. But I cannot allow them this false supposition. God is not to be understood as foreseeing something in them which procures grace for them; rather they are foreknown because they were freely chosen. Hence Paul elsewhere teaches the same thing: God knows them that are His (II Tim 2.19), because, that is, He holds them marked and as it were numbered in His roll. Nor is the point omitted by Augustine:[1] the term foreknowledge is[2] to be taken as meaning the counsel of God by which He predestines His own to salvation. No one denies that it was foreknown by God who were to be heirs of eternal life. The real question is whether what He foresees is what He will make of them or what they will be in themselves. It is a futile subtlety to seize on the word foreknowledge and to attach to the merits of man that election which Paul always ascribes to the purpose of God alone. Peter, too, salutes the elect as elect according to the foreknowledge of God (I Pet 1.2). Is this because some foreseen virtue in them inclined God's favour towards them? Not at all: Peter is not comparing men among themselves to make some better than others; he puts high above all causes the decree which God determined in Himself. It is as if he had said they are now to reckon themselves among the sons of God, because, before they were born, they had been elected. On this ground in the same chapter he teaches that Christ was foreordained before the foundation of the world to wash away the sins of the world by His sacrifice. Without a doubt this means that the expiation of sin executed by Christ was ordained by the eternal decree[3] of God. Nor can what is found in Peter's sermon recorded by Luke be otherwise explained: Christ was delivered to death by the determinate counsel and foreknowledge of God (Acts 2.23). Peter thus joins foreknowledge with counsel that we may learn that Christ is not driven to death by chance or by the violent assault of men,[4] but because God, the most good and wise knower of all things, had deliberately so decreed it. Indeed one passage from Paul suffices to put a stop to all controversy. God, he says, declines to repudiate His people whom He foreknew (Rom 11.2). And shortly after he declares what this knowledge was, that there was a remnant

---

[1] *De Dono Persever.*, cap. 18. [2] Chief authority erroneously has: not.
[3] Beza has: *consilio* (instead of: *scito*).
[4] French adds: as if He had been constrained to suffer their will.

saved according to the election of grace (v. 5). He says again
(v. 7) that Israel did not by works obtain what it sought, but
election did obtain it. What he called foreknowledge in the
first passage, he afterwards defines as election—and that
gratuitous.

V.2. The Fourth Gospel

It is a puerile fiction by which Pighius interprets grace to
mean that God invites all men to salvation despite their being
lost in Adam. For Paul clearly distinguishes the foreknown from
the others upon whom God did not please to look. The same
thing is expressed as plainly in the words of Christ: Whatever
the Father gives Me shall come to Me; and him who comes to
Me I shall not throw out (Jn 6.37). Here we have three things
briefly but clearly expressed: first, all that come to Christ were
given to Him by the Father before; second, all who were given
are transmitted from the Father's hand to His, so that they may
be truly His; and lastly, He is a faithful custodian of all whom
the Father entrusted to His good faith and protection, so that
none is allowed to perish. Now if the question of the beginning
of faith be raised, Christ replies: Those who believe believe
because they were given to Him by the Father. The incredulity
of the scribes was a great obstacle[1] to the ignorant people,
because people were persuaded that no doctrine was worthy of
belief except what had received their sanction. Christ on the
other hand declares that the light by which we are directed
into the way of salvation is solely the gift of God. Anyone can
deny that those whom the Father chose in Him are given to
Christ;[2] nevertheless it remains a fixed fact that the gift is not
only prior to faith but its cause and origin. To the other clause
there attaches much greater weight. For here He declares not
only that none come to Him except those to whom the hand of
the Father is held out, but also that all given by the Father
without exception believe. No one, He says, can come to Me,
unless my Father draw him (Jn 6.44). Pighius himself will confess that illumination is needed if those who are at enmity with
God are to turn to Christ. But at the same time he imagines that
grace is offered equally to all, and that in the last resort it is by
the will of man as each is willing to receive it, that it is rendered

---

[1] French has: scandal.

[2] French adds: and that by this means He gives Him those who believe.

efficacious. But Christ Himself testifies that the sense of His words is different: There are some among you who do not believe. Therefore I said to you that no man is able to come to Me, unless it is given him by My Father (v. 64f.). You see here that Christ excludes the unbelieving from the number of those who are drawn. For this would have been inappropriately said, if faith were not a special gift. But clearest of all is what He says after quoting the prophet Isaiah: They shall all be taught by God (Is 54.13; Jn 6.45); for He immediately adds by way of interpretation: Every one who has heard and learned of My Father comes to Me. In this He teaches the prophecy of Isaiah is fulfilled, that God inwardly addresses His disciples by His Spirit, so that He may deliver them into the possession of Christ. Isaiah defines this as the method of renewing the Church, that all His sons are divinely instructed. He records therefore a special benefit of which God deems worthy none but the sons of the Church. By this kind of teaching, Christ declares that those are efficaciously drawn to Him whose minds and hearts God compels. For so, says Augustine,[1] He teaches those within who are called according to His purpose, at the same time giving them both to know what they ought to do and also to do what they know. But he who knows what he ought to do and does not do it, has not yet learned of God according to grace, but only according to law, not according to the spirit but to the letter. A little later:[2] If, as the truth says, everyone that learns comes, everyone who does not come has certainly not learned. Finally he concludes: It does not follow that he who can come really does come, unless he is willing and comes. But everyone who has learned of the Father is not only able to come but really does come; for there is now present the possibility of coming forward, the motion of the will and the effect of the act. Nor do I adduce the testimony of Augustine thus in order to fight under his authority, but because words more apt than his are not available with which to express the mind of the evangelist. Should there be any who do not yet acquiesce, he elsewhere[3] discusses the matter more fully. Thus, Christ says: Everyone who has heard and learned of the Father comes to Me. What does this mean, unless: There is no one who hears

[1] *De Gratia Christi contra Pelag. et Coelest.*, lib. I, cap. 13.
[2] Ibid., cap. 14.
[3] *De Praedest. Sanct.*, cap. 8.

and learns of the Father, and does not come to Me? For if
everyone who has heard and learned of the Father comes, it
follows that everyone who does not come has neither heard nor
learned of the Father. For if he had heard and learned, he
would come. This school of God is certainly far from the
understanding of the flesh; in it the Father teaches and is heard,
so that a man may come to the Son. A little later, Augustine
declares: This grace which is secretly communicated to human
hearts is received by no heart that is hardened. Indeed it is
given for the purpose of first taking away his hardness of heart.
When therefore the Father is inwardly heard, He takes away
the stony heart and gives the heart of flesh. Thus He makes
sons of promise and vessels of mercy prepared for glory. Why
then does He not teach all men so that they may come to Christ,
unless because all He teaches He teaches in mercy, but those
He does not teach He does not teach in judgment? For He has
mercy on whom He will have mercy, and whom He wills He
hardens. The sum of this matter may, however, be compressed
into even smaller compass. Of those drawn to the Father,
Christ does not say that a flexible heart is given to them, but
that God touches their heart inwardly by His Spirit so that by
this means they come. That this is not given promiscuously to
all, experience demonstrates even to the blind.

Now Christ declares that He casts out no one of this number,
but rather that their life rests in safety, until He raises them in
the last day. Who does not see that this final perseverance, as
it is commonly called, is similarly ascribed to the election of
God? It may be that some fall from faith. But Christ affirms that
those given to Him by the Father are placed beyond the peril
of destruction. Similarly at another place (Jn 10.26ff.), having
said that some of the Jews did not believe, because they are not
of His sheep, He places the sheep themselves, as it were, in a
safe haven of salvation. They shall never perish, He says, nor
shall anyone pluck them out of My hand. The Father who gave
them to Me is greater than all. Pighius will not dare to base so
safe a state of salvation upon their present faith; yet he makes
it depend upon the freewill of man.[1] Nor must we think it an
ambiguous and discussable point when Christ opposes His
protection alone against all the devices of Satan, or declares
us to be safe up to the end, because He wills to save us. So that

---

[1] French adds: or rather that it hangs on this as on a thread.

no doubt may remain about whom in His faithfulness He undertakes to protect, He again recalls us to the gift of the Father. Nor should it be lightly overlooked that Christ makes the Father greater than all possible adversaries, lest we should have less security of salvation than reverence for the power of God. Hence in all violent assaults, all kinds of peril, all mighty storms and agitations, the perpetuity of our standing consists in this, that God will constantly defend with the strength of His arm what He has decreed in Himself concerning our salvation. If anyone of us should regard himself, what can he do but tremble? For everything around us shakes, and nothing is more feeble than ourselves. But since the heavenly Father allows none of those whom He has given to His Son to perish, our assurance and confidence are as great as His power. For He is so mighty that He stands the constant and invincible vindicator of His gift. For as Augustine wisely says:[1] If any of these should perish, God would be deceived. But none of them perish, because God is not deceived. If any of these should perish, God is conquered by the sin of man. But none perish, because God is conquered by nothing. For they are elected to reign with Christ perpetually, not like Judas to a temporal office for which he was fitted. And again:[2] Of these none perishes, because all are elect, and this not according to their own purpose but to God's; seeing that there is conferred upon them, as he later says, not such a gift of perseverance as makes them able if they will, but as can do nothing but persevere. This he confirms by very good reason. In the weakness of this life there is indeed need of strength effectively to repress pride. But if in this weakness men were left only their own will, in such a way that if they willed they might remain within the power of God (without which they could not persevere) without God working in them that will, then the will itself amid so many great trials would succumb under its own weakness. Thus men would not be able to persevere at all; for, failing under their weakness, they would either not be willing or would not so will as to be able. Therefore help is offered to the weakness of the human will, so that it is moved undeviatingly and inseparably by divine grace, and hence though infirm it does not fail, nor is it overcome by any weakness.

[1] *De Corrept. et Grat.*, cap. 7.
[2] Ibid., cap. 12.

V.3. Romans 9

There must now be adduced that memorable passage from Paul which alone ought easily to compose all controversy among sober and compliant children of God. It is no wonder if that Cyclops Pighius ridicules the words contemptuously;[1] yet I hope I shall bring all sound readers to abhor such barbarous and audacious profanation of Scripture. As the Jews, priding themselves on the title Church, repudiated the gospel on the pretext that it had been condemned by this fictitious Church, lest the majesty of the gospel should be overshadowed by such shameless pride, Paul tears aside the mask behind which they boast.[2] It was certainly a formidable obstacle for the weak to see the teaching of Christ rejected by all those whom God had appointed heirs of His eternal covenant. The apostles preached that Jesus was the Messiah of God. The whole nation to which the Messiah had been promised repudiated Him. Is it any wonder, then, if today we see many wavering before the transient deceit of the Papists who boast themselves to be the Church?[3] Paul therefore comes to grips with the Jews in this way. He makes out that the fleshly seed are by no means the legitimate children of Abraham; the children of promise are alone reckoned among the seed (Rom 9.8). He could have counted the seed on the basis of faith. This would have been consistent when he was stating the distinction within the promise between genuine and spurious; and this he has already done (capp. 2 and 4). But now he rises higher: those are children of promise whom God elected before they were born. For he cites what was promised to Abraham by the angel (Gen 18.10): In due time I shall come and Sarah will have a son. This is as if he said: Before he was conceived in the womb, Isaac was chosen by God. He continues: More than this; when, from one embrace of our father Isaac, Sarah conceived, while the children were not yet born nor had done good or evil, so that the purpose of God according to election might stand, not in works, but in Him who calls, it was said: The elder will serve

[1] French has: How the despisers of God advance objections to obscure and confuse everything! Yet I hope, etc.

[2] French adds: showing that it is a frivolous arrogance in them to usurp the name of Church for themselves.

[3] It was certainly . . . Church—this section omitted in French.

the younger, as it is written, Jacob have I loved, but Esau have I hated (Rom 9.11ff.).

Pighius[1] puts up the excuse that this is one of the most difficult passages in Scripture. Let this be conceded; I am thereby far from allowing that his impious barking is tolerable when he asseverates that the labyrinth is inextricable. What? are we to say that the Spirit speaking by the mouth of Paul slipped, so as to lead us away beyond what is useful?[2] It would have been easy for him, as I have said, to distinguish the true from the spurious children of Abraham[3] simply by the mark of faith. But he intentionally raises the question of election, which is a much more profound question. He records that, when caught up above the third heaven, secrets were revealed to him which it is not lawful for a man to utter (II Cor 12.2). Therefore, it is manifest enough that he was aware how far it is both expedient and lawful to go in publishing the secrets of God. Since then he takes to such a high level a question which could be settled in popular and brief terms, what godly man will hesitate to show himself docile and attentive? Unless of course[4] it were to be hoped that our furious Cyclops would restrict by his moderation the Spirit of God from trespassing beyond due limits! He adds: This is one of the passages which uninstructed and unstable men corrupt to their own destruction. This very thing he compels us to confess of him, he himself extorting this conclusion by the plainest proof, so lawlessly does he twist and pervert Paul's whole context. When he exhorts his readers to hold themselves obedient to the Church in these obscurities and for the interpretation of difficult passages, he would have my support too, if only he showed them a sheepfold of Christ and not a stinking sty of swine. For what is the Church of Pighius but the conglomeration of all impieties, the whirlpool filled with all errors and still insatiable? His last admonition is that his readers should admit nothing inconsistent with the

---

[1] Lib. 9, cap. 2.

[2] French adds: and plunge us in darkness instead of instructing us.

[3] French has: the dissemblers and false pretenders.

[4] Unless of course . . . unambiguously means—French runs quite differently: In brief, if we refuse to accept what he shows us, this is plainly to disdain to receive what is shown to us by the Spirit of God. We shall later see what opportunity the wicked have of grumbling against what does at first sight seem strange. For the present, let us be content to learn in the school of God, knowing that He is so good a master that all that we get from Him will be profitable for our salvation.

immense goodness of God, nor anything that incites them to hate rather than to love Him. But here he runs full sail against God for determining some from their very creation to destruction. Yet even if all this doctrine be suppressed, the reprobate would never lack occasion for holding God in detestation and for attacking Him with their sacrilegious arguments. What reason there is for their opposition will be considered in its proper place, when the mind of Paul has been expounded. For the present let all who can bear to be taught in the school of God hear what Paul plainly and unambiguously means.

He puts before us the two sons of Isaac, who, when they were equally begotten in nature's sacred womb as in a temple of God, were none the less separated to dissimilar lots by the oracle of God. The cause of discrimination, which might otherwise be sought in the merits of each, Paul assigns to the hidden[1] counsel of God, that the purpose of God might stand. We learn that it was determined by God that one only of these two twins be elected. These words of Paul, Pighius tries to root up with a foolish objection, like a hog with its snout.[2] He replies[3] that the election of grace means that Jacob had not merited any such things. But Paul commends grace because one is elected while the other is rejected. Hence what Pighius supposes about universal grace falls immediately to the ground. Paul does not simply teach that Jacob is nominated the heir of life in order that the election of God might stand, but that, his brother being set aside, the birthright was conferred on him. I do not indeed forget what other dogs bark out, what are also the objections of the ignorant, that the testimony cited from Paul[4] does not deal with eternal life and eternal destruction. But if these objectors held the true principles of theology which ought to be well known to all Christians, they would speak a little more modestly. For the answer given to Rebecca showed her that the issue of the struggle she felt in her womb would be that the blessing of God and the covenant of eternal life would remain the possession of the younger. For what did the struggle itself mean except that both could not at the same time be heirs of the covenant which was already in the secret counsel of God destined for one? They object that the covenant referred to the

[1] French has: closely hidden.   [2] French omits this sentence.
[3] French has: they are constrained to mean.
[4] French has: from Moses and the prophet Malachi (Rom 9.12).

land of Canaan, about which the word of Malachi also speaks (Mal 1.2).[1] Here they might perhaps be listened to, if God had fattened the Jews in the land of Canaan like pigs in a sty. The thought of the prophet is very different. For God had promised that land as an external symbol[2] of a greater inheritance and had given it for a possession to his posterity, so that He might gather them as a people peculiar to Himself, and might erect a sanctuary[3] and testimony of His presence and grace. These are the ends that the prophet fitly ponders. In a word, he represents the land of Canaan as the sacred domicile of God. Since Esau is deprived of this habitation, he understands him to be hated of God; for he was rejected from the holy and elect family in which the love of God perpetually resides. We also must consider the nature with which God has invested that land, that it should be an earnest and pledge of the spiritual covenant with the seed of Abraham into which God entered. Hence, it is very relevant that Paul should record (Rom 9.12) the gratuitous election settled on Jacob, because, being not yet born, and his brother being rejected, he is appointed to enjoy the inheritance. But Paul proceeds even further. This dignity was not obtained by all: the brothers are separated before either had done anything either good or evil. Hence he concludes that the discrimination was carried out on the basis not of works but of Him who calls.

Here Pighius obtrudes upon us that noisome distinction of his. Works already done did not indeed come into consideration, for there were none; but the election of God was ratified on Jacob because God foresaw his faith and obedience. And he philosophises[4] ingeniously upon the name of Israel, saying that he was so named from seeing God, so that we may know that they are indeed true Israelites who, being not blind from their own wickedness but only with respect to God, open their eyes to see God when He appears to them. But is it not ridiculous that, while concerned to make others so clear-sighted, he himself should be blinder than a mole? An etymology entirely different is given by Moses, that he had wrestled with the angel of God and was victorious. For Israel means having power with God or prevailing over God.

---

[1] French has no reference to Malachi.   [2] French has: earnest and pledge.

[3] French has: the temple and ark of alliance.

[4] And he philosophises . . . prevailing over God—lacking in the French.

But whose eyes, I ask, will he be able so to close or tear out
that they will not notice his absurdities? Why does Paul deny
that they had done anything good or evil unless to remove all
consideration of merit?—why, unless precisely to affirm that
God drew His reasons from no source other than Himself, when
He passed so diverse a judgment upon the twin brothers? I
know that this is a common means of escape. But I would first
know, if Esau and Jacob had been left to their common nature,
what greater total of good works would God have found in the
second than in the first? Clearly the hardness of a stony heart
in both would have repudiated offered salvation. But, says
Pighius, a flexible heart was given to both that they might be
able to embrace grace; but the one by his free will willed to do
what he could, while the other refused. As if Paul testified that
the unwillingness was also given by God! As if God did not
promise that Israel should walk in His precepts![1] But in the
judgment of Pighius, John (1.12) loudly denies that God has
given us power to become the sons of God. But this wild fellow
is deluded in thinking that power means faculty or ability,
when in fact it rather signifies title to the honour. He betrays a
more than gross dullness when, as with shut eyes, he disregards
the cause of this power which is described by the evangelist. He
declares that those become the sons of God who receive Christ,
but affirms immediately after that they are born not of flesh
and blood but of God. God therefore deems them worthy of the
honour of adoption who believe on His Son but whom before
He had begotten by His Spirit; that is, those He formed to be
sons of Himself, these He declares at last to be His. For if faith
renders us sons of God, it has to be considered from where it
derives. For it is the fruit of the seed of the Spirit by which God
begets us into newness of life. In a word, what Augustine says
is most true, that the redeemed are distinguished from the lost
by grace alone; and even them the common mass of original
corruption would have hardened into perdition. Hence, it
follows that the grace of God to be preached is that which
makes and does not find men elect. This is what he is always
insisting.[2] Add to this that, if God forsees anything in His elect

---

[1] French adds: The question here is not of a faculty of indifference but of an actual virtue.

[2] *Enchir. ad Laur.*, cap. 99; *Epist. ad Sixtum*, 105 (Migne 194); *Contra Iulianum*, lib. 5, cap. 3; and elsewhere.

for which He separates them from the reprobate, Paul would have argued foolishly in asserting that God's appointment: The elder will serve the younger, referred not to works but to Him that calls, because the brothers were not yet born. Hence the solution in terms of the foreseen works of each clearly insults Paul. He concludes that in the election of God there is no respect of works, because God preferred Jacob to his brother before they were born or had done anything good or evil. Opponents of this doctrine try to establish that those who are elect of God are distinguished by some mark of goodness from the reprobate; hence they make out that the matter depends upon some future disposition in each to receive or repudiate grace. Even if they accepted the expression, who had not yet done anything good, God would still not be disregarding works in electing them, because election would still depend on works foreseen by Him. But Paul regards as admitted fact what is incredible to these fine theologians, that all are equally unworthy and the nature of all equally corrupt. Hence he safely concludes that God elects those whom He elects in His gracious purpose, not those whom He foresaw would be obedient sons. Further, Paul is considering what the nature of man would be without the election of God; his opponents are dreaming of the good God foresaw in man which would never exist unless He Himself effected it.

Although these things are clear enough in themselves, yet the context leads us deeper. For there follows: What shall we then say? that there is unrighteousness with God? Either this objection is introduced without reason, or Paul's doctrine has no place for works foreseen. For what suspicion of unrighteousness can be conceived, where God offers grace equally to all but permits the worthy to enjoy it? In a word, when these objectors make the cause of election or reprobation future works, they appear to evade and solve for themselves the very question which Paul puts to them. Hence, it is manifest that he himself is not instructed in this new wisdom. Let it be that Paul introduces these opponents as quarrelling importunately and groundlessly about the justice of God. Note how he repudiates the objection. The words are: God forbid; for He says to Moses, I will have mercy on whom I will have mercy and compassion on whom I will have compassion. Nothing will, I see, be more fitting than to use the words of Augustine in

explaining this passage. It is marvellous, he says,[1] when hemmed
in by these straits to see the abyss into which they precipitate
themselves for fear of the net of truth. They say God hated one
of these unborn children and loved the other because He foresaw their future works. How remarkable that this acute understanding of the matter escaped the apostle! Yet he did not see
it, for he replies that the question raised here for himself and
his opponents is not to be solved with such brevity, with such
obvious truth, as they think. For in putting forward this
stupendous matter, how it could rightly be said that God loved
one and hated the other, he himself declares: What shall we
then say? is there unrighteousness with God? Now here was
the place for him to give the reason they have in mind:[2]
Because God foresaw their future works. But the apostle does
not say it. Rather, lest anyone should glory in the merits of his
own works, he wishes to commend the grace of God by estab-
lishing what God Himself has said. For He said to Moses: I
will have mercy on whom I will have mercy. Where are merits
now? where are works past or future, fulfilled or to be fulfilled
as by the free will of men?

Does not the apostle plainly declare his mind in commendation of gratuitous grace? Thus far I have considered the words
of Augustine. Let us suppose that Paul had said no such
thing.[3] How easy the solution would be! God discriminates
between men on the basis of future works. Why then does Paul
entangle himself deeper and assert that the whole cause is in
the will of God? For first the Lord vindicates to Moses His free
right to exercise mercy where He pleases, lest anyone should
dare to prescribe a law for Him. Then He declares that He will
take out of the whole multitude of the people those whom He
wished to deliver—and all were alike covenant-breakers. He
does not say the choice would depend on themselves, so that
He would be propitious to any whom He found worthy of
pardon. He precisely testifies that He is the arbiter of mercy,
so as to spare those whom He should will, for He is bound by
no necessity to elect one rather than another.

Paul goes on to infer what necessarily follows from this
statement: it is not of him that wills or him that runs, but of
God that shows mercy. For if the salvation of men is wholly

---

[1] *Epist. ad Sixtum*, 105 (Migne 194).
[2] French has: what these invent.   [3] French adds: and come to the facts.

comprehended within the mercy of God, and God saves none
but those whom in His secret good pleasure He chose, there is
nothing left over for man to do. Pighius' explanation is that
salvation is due to no endeavour of ours nor to any[1] works,
because God gratuitously calls us all to salvation. Of course
he plays about in safety, as if by a single word he could immediately dismiss Paul's whole doctrine. Paul's premise is: because
the Lord in His good pleasure saves whom He chooses, without
discimination of works; and his conclusion: therefore it is not
of him that wills nor him that runs, and the whole matter turns
on the mercy of God alone. Pighius thinks to make his escape
by talking of grace to all; whereas it is due to none. Then,
when he says that those become partakers of grace whom the
Lord finds fit and obedient to Himself, he necessarily falls back
on the acknowledgement that the willing and the running do
avail, but that, because by themselves they are not sufficient,
the palm has to be awarded to the grace of God. But Augustine
admirably refutes these absurdities. If, he says,[2] the reason
for the: Not of him that wills nor of him that runs but of God
who shows mercy, is that the matter depends on both, that is
both on the will of man and the mercy of God, then it follows
that will alone is not sufficient unless the grace of the Lord be
added, and that the grace of God is not sufficient unless the
will of man be added. Further, if no Christian will dare to say:
It is not of God that shows mercy but of man who wills, it
remains that the right understanding of the saying: Not of
him that wills nor of him that runs, is that all be ascribed to
God who both prepares the good will of man for help and
helps it when prepared. Even more frivolous is the cunning of
others who in this matter search out a concurrence of God's
grace and man's endeavour. As if Paul meant that men's
running effected little unless helped by the grace of God, and
did not rather intend to reduce all other things to nothing that
the place might be wholly vacated for the grace of God. For
whence is the principle of right running? Can anyone of himself go to meet God, unless led and directed by the Holy
Spirit? For, if I may use here also the words of Augustine:[3]
Every day there are drawn to Christ those who are His enemies.
For Christ says: No one can come to Me, unless the Father

---

[1] French, Beza and Amst. have: those.
[2] *Enchir. ad Laur.*, cap. 32.   [3] *Ad Bonif.*, lib. 1, cap. 19.

draw him. He does not say lead, as if willing somehow preceded; for who is drawn unless he is willing to go? He is therefore drawn in wonderful ways by Him who knows how to work in the hearts of men, not that men believe against their wills, but that the unwilling are made willing. We see therefore, that the election of God is ratified by the subsequent running of men, so that His mercy alone (which raises the fallen, brings the straying back into the way, raises the dead to life, and calls things that are not) may have pre-eminence.

There follows the other clause concerning the reprobate, of whom Paul finds the most signal instance in Pharaoh. Of him, God speaks thus to Moses: For this I have set thee up, to show My power in thee. Paul faithfully renders the passage word for word: For this I have raised thee up. The word used is the *hiphil* of the root *amad* which means to stand.[1] Pharaoh therefore is said to be introduced as one in whom God provides a memorable example of His power. Why does the Lord accept him and set him in this place? Pighius would have it that God sustained him by His patience for a time, though worthy of death.[2] Let me permit him this escape. Yet he is still entangled and caught by the fact that God destined Pharaoh to destruction and left him to his own devices. If Pighius commend the patience of God, I agree. Yet this remains an incontrovertible fact, that the reprobate are set aside in the counsel of God to the end that in them He might demonstrate His power. And this patience is far from Paul's mind, as appears in the next reference: Whom He wills He hardens. This would not have been added, unless by the term setting or raising up Paul had not meant the counsel of God by which He ordained Pharaoh by his stubbornness to illustrate the redemption of His people. For if anyone should say his being divinely raised up was to the summit of royal honour, this is indeed a part of the meaning, but not all. For the Greek interpreters used here the same word by which they were accustomed to render the *hiphil* derived from the root *kum*, which means to arise.[3] Further, God is said to raise up what He brings forward as with an outstretched arm for the end ordained in His counsel. But Scripture looks to the beginning

---

[1] Paul faithfully renders . . . stand—French omits.
[2] Beza and Amst. have: power.
[3] For the Greek interpreters . . . arise—French omits.

of the thing being done, that it may ascribe it to God alone. So God is said to raise up prophets and ministers of salvation, lest any of these be claimed for man on the ground of his industry. Hence the meaning of Moses was faithfully expressed by the word raised up, if only you will understand it thus;[1] and Paul did not understand it otherwise. Certainly the term comprehends both plainly and summarily what he touched on concerning the elect and the reprobate; for he claims for God the right and the power to harden and to have mercy according to His will. He declares the right to harden and to have mercy to be His, and that no law can be imposed upon Him as rule, because no law or rule better or more just than His will can be conceived. But because formerly some considered that Paul introduces impious objectors against God, Pighius, too, has resort to this refuge. Suppose this be permitted to him. The knot is not thus loosed. For Paul does not raise a question about nothing; and moreover, his reply is to admit as true what his adversaries object. What profit then[2] does Pighius derive from hesitation of this kind, except to show that his case is a bad one? Who will allow him what he asks, when he so violently separates what hangs together, and joins in one bundle what is clearly distinguished? After showing the reprobate and the elect to be discriminated by the incomprehensible[3] counsel of God, he infers in the same context: Therefore He has mercy on whom He will, and whom He will He hardens. To this he adds: You will then say to me: Why does He yet find fault? When Paul clearly distinguishes the disputing persons, must we not accept his words rather than the extraneous comments? For the rest, Augustine, here as often, makes a prudent observation: It matters little how exactly you come to accept what Paul's argument approves as true.[4]

If the objection had been false, it is certainly improbable that Paul in a cause so good, so clear and so plausible, would have been silent. For if it is false that God hardens whom He will, the knot, so inexplicable to human ingenuity, would easily have been loosed with one word. Pighius represents Paul as declining

---

[1] Hence the meaning . . . understand it thus—a version omits.

[2] French has more simply: For the rest, that is not to be separated which is joined together.

[3] French has: irreproachable.   [4] *Enchir. ad Laur.,* cap. 99.

to give a clear and fit reply because he did not regard impudent persons as worthy of reply, so that they might rather learn to know with humility than proudly demand a reason for the works of God. Thus, we read elsewhere that the Jews who asked Christ by what authority He did His works were repulsed by only a question in return. But the words of Paul contradict this. For afterwards he restrains the insolence of those who indulge a too audacious curiosity in investigating the secrets of God, but none the less confirms that the reprobate are vessels of His wrath in whom He shows His power. Augustine[1] is therefore a much better interpreter: When the question is asked: Why does He yet find fault? is Paul's reply: O man, what thou hast said is false? Not at all. The reply is: O man, who art thou? What Augustine elsewhere says is to be observed. Paul does not break off the argument with a reproof when they contend against God with sacrilegious petulance, as if the justice of God needed serious defence. He brings forward what is most expedient. Certain foolish persons think the apostle to have been deficient in his reply at this point, and to have simply repressed the audacity of his opponent for want of good reason. But the weight of what he says is great: O man, who art thou? In such questions, he recalls man to a consideration of his capacity. Only one brief word, but in fact the reason given is very weighty. For who can reply to God who does not accept it? and if he do accept it, he will find even less to reply, etc.[2]

Hence the same writer says elsewhere:[3] If such arguments move us because we are men, let us also listen when he says: O man, who art thou? And a little later: For though God did not create the sins of men, who but God created the natures of men themselves, which are undoubtedly good in themselves, but from which according to the decree of His will the evil of sin was destined to proceed, and in many such sins as would merit eternal punishment? Why? unless because He willed it. Why did He will it? O man, who art thou that repliest against God? Is there any other vain notion? Look, a reason is here offered to man that is sufficient for him, if indeed he will accept it who in the bondage of infirmity contends for the

[1] *De Praedest. Sanct.*, cap. 8.

[2] French has: For if we understand what it means to say: No one is able to reply to God, this ought to be enough for us. If we do not understand it, even less will we find it possible to plumb this profundity.

[3] *Epist. ad Bonif.*, 106 (Migne 186).

freedom of his own will. If the ill desire to contend with God still entices him, let such a man, says Augustine,[1] speak and hear as is proper for a man: O man who art thou? Let him hear and not despise. If anyone be a despiser, let him understand himself hardened to despise; if he be not a despiser, let him understand himself assisted not to despise—hardened according to desert, assisted according to grace. What the desert imputed to man is, Augustine had earlier showed in these words: Every sinner is inexcusable, either by original sin, or by the addition of his own will, whether he knows or is ignorant, whether despite right judgment or not. For ignorance itself in those who will not understand is undoubtedly sin, and in those unable to understand it is the punishment of sin.[2]

But to take no further help from the testimony of Augustine,[3] let my readers ponder the matter by itself with me. Paul, comparing man with God as he does here, shows that the counsel of God in electing and reprobating men is undoubtedly more profound and more deeply concealed than the human mind can attain. It is as if he said: Do you consider, O man, who you are, and allow more to God than the measure of your nature can compass. But let us give place to the philosophising of Pighius:[4] the condition of all men is equal, except in so far as some deprive themselves of eternal life though they like others were elected. Where then would be the difficulty and the obscurity? what would not be acceptable to common sense and plausible to natural judgment? When then you hear of a mystery surpassing the comprehension of human intelligence,[5] you may immediately conclude that solutions derived from common judgment, which might be valid in a secular court of justice, are frivolous. Pighius interposes here that none are repelled by the Lord nor sent away in suspense who humbly discipline their minds, and that this opposition to God is found only in the refractory and proud. To this I assent without difficulty; only let him on his side admit that Paul charges with impious pride all who measure the justice of God by their own

---

[1] *Epist. ad Sixtum*, 105 (Migne 104).   [2] French has: of original sin.

[3] French has: Let us take a case which Augustine did not consider, and leaving him aside consider the facts as they are.

[4] French has: Now if we accept this supposition that all are equal and none deprived of life unless, after being elected, they consciously withdraw from it; where then, etc.

[5] Beza and Amst. have: which is the supreme head of human intelligence.

comprehension. But on the judgment of Pighius, God must render a reason for whatever He does, if His justice is to win praise. The rule of modesty prescribed by us, on the other hand, is that, where the reason for God's works lies hidden, we none the less believe Him to be just. The son of Sirach[1] is not ashamed to extol God with the eulogy that as a potter He discriminates between His vessels according to His will, and that men are similarly in the hand of God who renders to them as He decrees. For κρίσις in this passage, if it is compared with what precedes, can mean nothing else than the good pleasure of the artificer. Nor do we need here any other interpreter, when Paul himself plainly rebukes the audacity of those who demand a reason of God. Is the clay to say to the artificer: Why have you made me? Hence to hold the will of God, though hidden, to be the highest justice and to allow Him the power of freely destroying and saving, is to limit oneself within the moderation prescribed by Paul. However Pighius may twist himself in twisting the words of Paul, the simile cannot be otherwise applied in the present instance than to show that God by His own right forms and fashions men to whatever destiny He wills. If this should seem absurd to anyone at first glance, he should recall the admonition of Augustine:[2] If beasts could speak and quarrel with their maker that they are not made men like us, all of us would be immediately enraged. What then do we think of ourselves? It is surely foolish not to ascribe to God a much greater excellency than that which He and all men possess over the beasts. Rightly expressed indeed, before God we are less than the beasts. What then remains but that the sheep of His flock quietly submit themselves to Him? This is much more fitting than to follow the example of Pighius in making men potters in the place of God, so that each contrives his own destiny by his own virtue. Elsewhere, he says, what is here obscure is made plain; for the furnace proves the potter's vessels and temptation those who are just. Hence he concludes that if a just man remains constant in faith and piety he will be a vessel to honour, and if he weakly fail he will be a vessel to dishonour. And since each by his own will, and assisted by divine grace prepared for all in common, does persevere, he concludes in the end that we are made vessels to honour by our invincible fortitude. I will not observe how foolishly two things

---

[1] See Wis. 15.7.   [2] *De Verbis Apost.*, sermo 11.

are here confused, the making of the vessel and its proving.[1] But I will observe that God's proving His own by various trials and conflicts does not at all prevent Him predestinating them in His eternal counsel before they were born for whatever use He pleased, nor making them such as He willed them afterwards to be. Nor does what Paul says help Pighius: If any man purify himself from evils of this kind, he will be a vessel to honour (II Tim 2.21). For Paul here discusses, not how men extricated from their baseness are made vessels to honour, but how the faithful already elect and called adapt themselves to pure uses.[2] Observe how exact is the harmony between Pighius and Paul! Pighius' words are: What he was silent about before, Paul here expresses, why God makes some vessels to honour and not others. So that Jacob might be a vessel of mercy, his soul had purified itself, and on the strength of this he was deservedly made a vessel of honour. God having regard to this purification which He foresaw chose him. Now listen to Paul. He is exhorting the faithful to purify themselves. To pave the way for this doctrine, he prefaces it: God knows them who are His (II Tim 2.19). Similarly elsewhere (Eph 2.10) he teaches that we are His workmanship, created unto good works, which also He has prepared. Paul then, who does not rashly boast of being a skilled architect,[3] lays this foundation for salvation, in the gratuitous election of God alone. Pighius on the contrary begins his building on the surface.[4] So too in dealing with the passage in Jeremiah, he uses many words to no purpose. The passage does not describe the origin of our formation; it asserts God's rightful power in the breaking and shattering of vessels already formed and finished. Paul's intention is to be observed. God the maker of men takes them from the same clay and forms them for honour or dishonour by His will (Rom 9.21); for He gratuitously chooses to life some not yet born, leaving others to that destruction which all by nature equally deserve. When Pighius denies that the

[1] French adds: St Paul treats here not of how we are proved but of how we are made.

[2] French has: give and devote themselves to conduct they know to be pleasing to God and fit for them who are instruments of His glory.

[3] French has: master builder and expert.

[4] French has: Those imagine that God chose each one according to what He foresaw in him, begin to build at window level and construct the ceiling before the foundations. We have then to note St Paul's intention (rest omitted).

election of grace has anything to do with hate of the reprobate, I quite agree that this is true; for to the gratuitous love with which the elect are embraced there corresponds on an equal and common level a just severity towards the reprobate.

Paul then concludes: What if God, willing to show His wrath and to make known His power, endured with great patience the vessels fitted for destruction, so that He might make known the riches of His grace towards the vessels of mercy which He prepared for glory? This supplies no cause of dispute against Him. As do others like him, Pighius plays with the word patience. Or rather he fiercely bandies it about, as if it were in paternal indulgence that God hardened the reprobate. In this way, he says, God forms vessels to dishonour by kindly enduring those who abuse His patience and accumulate a treasury of wrath against themselves. Where is then the difference between the brothers not yet born? If Pighius is to be believed, God foresaw Esau's future hardness of heart. How then is the election of grace so manifest in Jacob, when Esau was given the same status until he excluded himself from the number of the sons? But Pighius' hesitation is so entirely refuted by a brief sentence of Paul, that there is no need to go elsewhere to assemble arguments against it. Anyone even moderately acquainted with Scripture knows quite well in what sense the Hebrews used the terms vessels and instruments. When we read of instruments, it is necessary to presuppose God as the author and overruler of the whole action and His hand to be the director. Why then are some called vessels of wrath, unless because God exercises upon them His just severity which He withholds from others? And why are they made vessels of wrath? Paul answers, that in them God might show His wrath and power. He says they are fitted to destruction. When or how, except by first origin and nature? For the nature of the whole human race was corrupted in the person of Adam. Not that the higher counsel of God did not precede; but that from this fountain the curse of God takes its rise, and the destruction of the human race. For Paul testifies that God prepared vessels for the glory of His mercy. If this is the characteristic of the elect, the rest were fitted to perdition, because left to their own nature they were thereby devoted to certain destruction. The frivolous suggestion that they are thus fitted by their own wickedness is so foolish that it needs no notice. It is indeed true that the reprobate procure the wrath of God by their own depravity and daily hasten its falling on their heads. But it must be allowed by all that Paul here treats of the difference arising from the hidden judgment of God. He also says that the riches of God's grace are made known, while on the other hand the vessels of wrath rush upon destruction. Here there is nothing of what Pighius babbles, that grace is equal towards all and that the goodness of God is better illustrated by His enduring the vessels of wrath and suffering them to come to their own end. As for God's patience, the solution is immediately at hand. It is connected with His power, so that God does not only permit what is done, but overrules it by His virtue. This, as is known, Augustine too observes.[1]

V.4. The Covenant

On no other ground can that contract of God stand inviolable: I am a jealous God, merciful to a thousand generations and a severe avenger unto the third and fourth generation (Ex 20.5ff.), except the Lord in His free will decree to whom He will show grace and whom He wills to remain devoted to eternal death. He extends grace to a thousand ages. Now, I ask, does God estimate the sons of the pious on their own merits when He continues to them the grace exhibited to their fathers on no other ground than that He had promised to do so? To Abraham, who had deserved nothing, He gratuitously binds Himself in faithfulness to be a God of grace to his posterity. Hence that solemn entreaty after his death:[2] Remember, O Lord, thy servant Abraham. Here certainly there is a selection between men, not on the merits of each, but on the covenant with the fathers. Not that all the posterity of Abraham descended from him according to the flesh possesses this privilege; but both the faith and the salvation of all those who out of the seed of Abraham are chosen for life are to be referred to this promise. Exactly similar is the nature of that vengeance which God executes unto the third and fourth generation. For the allegation of some, that those who sin from age to age are punished each in his own order, is worse than frivolous. So formerly the Pelagians, unable to extricate themselves from the testimonies of Scripture which all show that all

[1] *Contra Iulianum*, lib. 5, cap. 5.
[2] French has: this fashion of praying customary to the faithful in the old dispensation.

men sinned in Adam, used to protest that all sinned by imitation. Just as then pious doctors attacked them, saying truly that all were condemned on account of the guilt of Adam from which the grace of Christ looses them, so in the present case it is necessary, if the parallel is to be maintained, to hold that God avenges in the person of the children the sins He condemned in their fathers. Nor can many other passages of Scripture be intelligibly explained otherwise, where God declares that He casts up the sins of the fathers into the bosom of their children (Ex 34.7; Deut 5.9; Jer 32.18). In vain do opponents object the passage in Ezekiel (18.2ff.): The son shall not bear the iniquity of the father, but the soul that sins shall die. For it is one part of vengeance that the Lord leaves men deprived and destitute of His Spirit, so that it comes about that each sustains his own punishment. Hence the children are said to bear the sins of their elders not undeservedly (as the profane poet sings);[1] for they are guilty on this very ground that, being by nature the sons of wrath as Paul says (Eph 2.3), being left to their own capabilities, being heirs from their first origin of eternal death, they can do nothing but constantly and unremittingly augment their own destruction.

V.5. Isaiah 6.9

Here it is opportune to expound the passage in Isaiah (6.9) which the Holy Spirit saw fit relevantly to repeat six times in the New Testament (Jn 12.40; Mt 13.14; Mk 4.12; Acts 28.25; Lk 8.10; Rom 11.8). The prophet is sent out with an apparently ominous mandate. Go and tell this people: Hear indeed, but do not understand; and see indeed, but do not perceive. Make fat the heart of this people, make heavy their ears, and close their eyes; lest they should perhaps see with their eyes, hear with their ears, understand with heart, and be converted for Me to heal them. That the prophet is called the minister of blindness, is, in my view, accidental. The real question turns upon the cause of the blindness. Also, I hold that it is a deserved punishment inflicted on a rebellious people, that for it light should be turned to darkness. Clearly a malicious and obstinate unbelief had preceded, which God requited with such a recompense.[2] But the prophet afterwards testifies that

---

[1] Horace, *Odes*, III, 6.1.

[2] French adds: should it be that the question is not again solved.

there was a certain chosen number upon whom salvation
shone from the word of God. The question therefore is whether
these escaped that terrible judgment by their own virtue or
were held safe by the hand of God. There is another even more
pressing question: How did it come about that out of that
multitude in which there was equal unbelief some were recovered, while the disease of others was incurable? If anyone
should judge the matter by human standards, the cause will
be looked for in the men themselves. But God does not allow
us to stop there. He declares all those who do not follow the
common defection are saved by His grace.[1] Whether recovery
is His own work ought not to be matter of controversy. What
Augustine says[2] is therefore evidently true: They are converted
to the Lord whom He Himself wills to be converted; for He
not only makes willing ones out of unwilling but also sheep
out of wolves and martyrs out of persecutors, reforming them
by more powerful grace. If the wickedness of men be urged
against this as cause,[3] it might indeed be more powerful than
such grace as God shows towards the elect, but for that one
truth: He has mercy on whom He will have mercy. And Paul's
interpretation leaves no doubt remaining (Rom 11.7). For
after saying that the election of God was determined, he adds
that the rest were blinded that the prophecy might be fulfilled.
I admit that the blindness was voluntary and freely acknowledge
their sin. But I note whom Paul excepts—those whom it
pleased God to elect. But why these rather than those? Lest
it vex us that choice of this kind is made, Paul says that men
have no right to contend against God.[4] So again elsewhere
(Acts 28.25), to the Jews, whose virulent malice he had experienced, he says: Well did the Holy Spirit speak by the mouth
of Isaiah, You will hear with your ears and not understand,
thus accusing them as they merited. Someone will wrongly
and ignorantly gather from this that the beginning of obduracy

[1] French adds: I have, says He, kept for myself seven thousand men who have
not at all bent the knee before the idol Baal.

[2] *De Praedest. Sanct.*, cap. 2.

[3] French has: If it be objected that men's wickedness resists the grace of God,
and denied that grace is such that He who promises it to His elect will have greater
efficacy and virtue than all wickedness and so surmount it, this would allow no
place for what He said by Moses: I will have mercy, etc.

[4] French has: We must not be too proud to reiterate a thousand times to those
who complain thus against God: O man, who art thou? As also St Augustine shows
(*De Dono Persever.*, cap. 12).

was their wickedness. As if there were not a cause deeper than that wickedness—the corruption of their nature; as if they did not remain sunk in this corruption because, reprobate by the secret counsel of God before they were born, they were not delivered from it.[1]

V.6. John 12.37ff.

Now let us listen to John, who will be no ambiguous interpreter (Jn 12.37ff.). Though Jesus had done many signs, he says, they did not believe; that the saying of Isaiah (53.1) might be fulfilled: Lord who has believed our report, and to whom is the arm of the Lord revealed? For this reason they could not believe, as Isaiah again says (6.9): He blinded their eyes, etc. Here certainly John does not record that the Jews were prevented by their wickedness from believing. While this was very true, yet he takes the matter higher. Here is to be seen the counsel of God. It disturbed the ignorant and weak in no small degree to hear that Christ had no place in the people of God. John replies that none believe except those to whom it is given; and there are few to whom God reveals His arm. This other prophecy on which the question now turns, he later weaves into the argument to the same end. And what he here inserts has great weight: they were not able to believe. Men may torture themselves as long as they wish; yet the cause of the discrimination, why God does not reveal His arm to all, lies hidden in His eternal decree. The intention of the evangelist is quite different. Faith is a special gift, and the wisdom of Christ is too lofty to fall within human understanding. Hence the unbelief of the world should not astonish us, even if the most acute lack faith. Hence,[2] unless we wish to evade what the evangelist confessedly contends, that few receive the gospel, we must conclude this to be established, that the external sound of the voice strikes our ears in vain, until God inwardly touches the heart.

For the other three evangelists (Mt 13.11; Mk 4.12; Lk 8.10), there is a different occasion for citing this passage. In Matthew, Christ separates His disciples from the crowds. He declares that it is given to them to know the mysteries of the

---

[1] See Aug., *Ad Bonif.*, lib. 2, cap. 6.

[2] French has: Hence, if we will not ridicule our knowledge of the Spirit of God, let us turn away from subterfuges for escaping from what the evangelist says, etc.

kingdom of heaven, and that He speaks to others in parables, that hearing they might not hear and that the saying of Isaiah might be fulfilled. I do not deny that those whom Christ addressed thus enigmatically and unprofitably were unworthy of greater light. But on the other hand, I would ask, in what way the apostles were more worthy of being admitted into familiarity with Christ? The antithesis stands: grace is conferred on few, when it could with equal right be denied to all. Shall we say that the disciples procured for themselves what the Lord asserts was given them? Nor is it to be lightly overlooked that He calls the things He spoke to them mysteries. And certainly there is nothing in all spiritual doctrine which does not much surpass and far exceed the comprehension of our mind.

Hence, no verbal explanation, however lucid, is enough, unless the Spirit teach us at the same time. But Christ wished it to be regarded by His disciples as a pledge[1] of rare dignity that in the external means of teaching He should honour them above the crowds. Meantime He gradually led them to the singular privilege which distinguishes members of the household from those outside, so that, taught from above, they might comprehend the things that are higher than natural understanding. Hence Christ's appeal: Who has ears to hear, let him hear (Mt 13.9; Lk 8.8). With these words, He not only distinguished the attentive from the inattentive hearers; He implies that all are deaf except those whose ears are pierced by the Lord (Ps 40.7). This benefit David celebrates in the name of the whole Church.[2] I shall not examine further isolated passages. Let this summary suffice. If we admit the Spirit of God who spoke by the apostle to be interpreter of the prophet, the hidden and incomprehensible judgment of God is to be adored even while it blinds the larger part of men lest seeing they should see. Here let all reasonings that can enter our minds cease. For if we confine ourselves to men, this will first be certain, that the Lord gives liberally to those who ask, and others waste away in their need for which they do not seek remedy. But unless there comes to our aid what Augustine says,[3] that it is of the divine beneficence not only to open to those that knock, but also to cause them to knock and ask, we

[1] French has: privilege.
[2] French has: which David shows to be peculiar to the children of God.
[3] *De Dono Persever.*, cap. 23.

shall never sufficiently know the need under which we labour. As for the help God gives, experience proves that all do not understand the power of the Spirit by which that is done which ought to be done. Let no one deceive himself with vain flattery. Those who come to Christ were sons of God in His heart when in themselves they were enemies of His. Because they were foreordained to life, they were given to Christ.[1] Hence, as Augustine faithfully admonishes,[2] let them remember that they are vessels of grace, not of merit; for grace is to them the whole of merit. Nor let us take pleasure in any other knowledge than that which is comprehended in admiration. Let those deride us who will, if only God in heaven nods in approval of us and the angels applaud.

VI. Pighius' Arguments

We shall now summarily gather such of Pighius' objections as have any plausibility, so that our readers may understand that the weapons with which he fights are no better than the cause for which he evoked such a great conflict. He says[3] that the whole question turns on this: To what end was man created? And first, he holds it as very absurd to suppose that God expected any return out of the creation of man; for God being self-contained lacks nothing. I indeed admit that God has no need of any external support; but I say it is an ignorant conclusion to draw from this that He has no regard for Himself in making men for His own glory. For what is the meaning of that word of Solomon (Prov 16.4): The Lord has made all things for Himself? Hence there is nothing absurd in saying that, though He lacked nothing, He yet created the race of men for His own glory. And this ought deservedly to be considered the chief end of man. The sophism of Pighius is the more ridiculous when he reasons that God was moved by no regard to His own glory in the creation of man because He is most perfect in Himself. But it is worth attention to hear how he extricates himself from that passage of Solomon: God made all things for Himself; but the reference is not to His own glory but on account of the immensity of His goodness. And lest this exposition should lack weight, he denies that any interpreters

---

[1] See Aug., *De Corrept. et Gratia*, cap. 5; also cap. 8 and 9.
[2] Ibid., cap. 7.   [3] Lib. 8, cap. 2.

agree with me, except a few detestable heretics, as he calls them.[1] Why should I spend time refuting such futile frivolities?[2] The Hebrew word *lammaanehu*[3] which Solomon uses means the same as if he said: for His own sake. This man, inflated with semi-Latin garrulity explains what the word *propter* means. But had he a spark of sanity, the context itself would plainly show that the wicked were created for the day of evil simply because God willed to illustrate His own glory in them; just as elsewhere He declares that Pharaoh was raised up by Him that He might show forth His name among the Gentiles (Ex 9.16). Further,[4] to give plausibility to his absurd error, he adduces the testimony of Moses: Now, Israel, what does the Lord thy God demand of thee but to love and worship Him? I trust that none of my readers is so silly as not see that we have here a man wanting in intellect and chattering without shame. What? does God will to be worshipped by us more for the sake of our good than His? is respect for His own glory so buried that He regards us alone? And what then is to be done with the testimonies of Scripture that establish the glory of God as the chief and ultimate end of man's salvation? Hence this principle must be held fast: God had such regard to our salvation as not to forget Himself but to set His own glory in the first place, and the whole world is constituted for the end of being a theatre of His glory. Not that He was not content with Himself or had need to borrow anything from elsewhere, but that He dignified His creatures with honour by impressing on them the plain marks of His glory (Eph 1.6).

Having made so dexterous a beginning, Pighius subjoins another end. God, having regard to the nature of His own goodness, wished to make a rational creature capable of receiving it; and this could not be done without the bestowal of freewill. If this is admitted, he thinks it is the ruin of what I teach. The discrimination between elect and reprobate cannot then be determined by the eternal decree of God, because man is arbiter of his future condition and has either fortune in his

[1] Lib. 7, cap. 2.

[2] And lest this exposition . . . frivolities—lacking in the French.

[3] So Amsterdam; other principal editions and Beza: *lamaannihu*; Gallasius: *jamaannihu*; French: The word which Solomon uses, for His own sake, carries quite another sense. And in fact what follows sufficiently shows that the wicked, etc. (rest omitted).

[4] Further . . . regards us alone—French omits.

hand. Here readers must be first warned and exhorted to hold
God, their maker and creator, in the honour due to Him, not
to obtrude with bold eyes to consider His purpose in creating
the human race, but to regard Him reverently, soberly and
with the clear eyes of faith. I know that hardly anything can
be said about the eternal predestination of God without many
perverse and absurd suppositions immediately creeping into
the mind. For this reason, there are some modest people who
would suppress all mention of the doctrine, lest material be
offered to undisciplined minds for exalting themselves. But I
must pass over such too nice speculations and leave them to
others. I do not think it right to shun the honest confession of
the truth lest it be exposed to the grimaces of the impious.
For nothing is more precious to God than His truth; nor does
He will that His justice be protected by our dissimulation, as
if He stood in need of such patronage.[1] We shall later deal with
this at greater length. Now I shall reply briefly to the point
at issue. Pighius contends that men were so immediately
created for salvation that no counsel of God concerning the
contrary event of destruction preceded. As if indeed the Lord
had not foreseen before the first man was made what the
future of the whole race would be! As if He had not decreed
what He wished to be done. That he might be the image of
God, man from the beginning was endowed with the light of
reason and rectitude of nature. Therefore God, as if blind,
awaited the outcome in doubt and suspense. Such is Pighius'
reasoning.[2] From this he boldly infers that God so disposed all
men at their creation without distinction or discrimination to
be partakers of His goodness and blessedness. But godly minds
cannot by this reasoning reconcile the two matters, that man
when first made was set in such a position that by voluntarily
falling he should be the cause of his own destruction, and yet
that it was so ordained by the admirable counsel of God that
this voluntary ruin to the human race and all the posterity of
Adam should be a cause of humility. For, though it pleased
God to arrange things so, yet man did not the less precipitate
voluntarily his own destruction though formerly endowed with
an upright nature and made in the image of God. I again repeat, I am aware how much absurdity and contradiction these

[1] French has: defence or excuse.
[2] Such is . . . blessedness—wanting in the French.

things carry with them for profane men. But, over against a
thousand witnesses, the voice of one conscience ought to
suffice for us.[1] If we listen to it, we shall be ashamed to deny
that man perished justly for voluntarily preferring to follow
Satan rather than God.

VII. Pighius' Proofs

Now let us hear Pighius' proofs. In them he tries to show that
salvation was ordained for all without distinction. Otherwise,
he says, the Spirit speaks falsely when declaring that God is the
Father of all. Malachi there (2.14) is dealing with marriage,
many husbands at that time being unfaithful in deceiving their
first wives with later polygamy. He recalls them to God as
author and avenger of conjugal fidelity.[2] Readers should note
how much religion Pighius manifests in dealing with Scripture.
He adds from the Psalm:[3] The Lord is good to all; and concludes that all without exception are destined to eternal life. If
this be true, the kindgom of heaven is open to dogs and donkeys.
For the prophet there does not praise the goodness of God
proper to man only but includes all the words of God. And why
should not Pighius fight on behalf of his brothers? There follows
a third proof. According to Paul (Rom 10.12), there is no
difference between Jew and Gentile. This I willingly accept;
only let there be added what the same Paul teaches: the
Gentiles were called to participation in the Gospel because
they had been ordained to it in the eternal counsel of God
(Rom 16.26). He cites also the passage from Ecclesiasticus:
God hates nothing which He made.[4] As if we were not always
saying that God hated nothing in us that is His, but only that
degenerate nature which is rightly considered a deformity of
the first creation. For the rest, the question of reprobation does
not at all turn on this hinge, whether God hated anything which
He made. For though God for secret reasons had decreed before
the defection of Adam what He would do, yet we read in
Scripture that nothing is condemned by Him except sin. It
remains that God had just causes for reprobating part of mankind, though they are hidden from us; but He hates and

---

[1] French has: whatever he prates or prattles. . . . Now let each one of you hear
what conscience says. . . .

[2] French adds: the better to show the enormity of their sin . . . and so make
them realise that they must show better fidelity and humanity to one another.

[3] Is the allusion to Ps 34.9?   [4] This appears in Wis 11.24.

condemns nothing in man except what is alien to His justice. He adds this from Paul: God included all under sin that He might have mercy on all (Rom 11.32; Gal 3.22). As if Paul here were discussing the number of men, and not rather simply praising the grace of God towards all who come to salvation! Certainly he intended nothing less than to extend the mercy of God to all. Rather he wishes to lay low all glorying in the flesh, so that we may know that no one will be saved except whom God saves by pure grace. Look then at the arguments by which Pighius shows that none are chosen from above to salvation in preference to others. Yet in the several titles of his chapters, he gives himself out for a not unskilled imitator of Euclid![1]

The passage from Solomon expresses well and clearly a third end for which God created all things for Himself: even the impious for the day of evil (Prov 16.4). This Pighius attacks thus. If we say God had respect to what would happen to each man, we must also admit that the discrimination between elect and reprobate was in the divine mind before the fall of man; hence it will follow that the reprobate are condemned not because they were ruined in Adam, but because before Adam's fall they were devoted to destruction. I reply that it is no wonder that Pighius should indiscriminately (to use his own word) confuse everything in the judgments of God, when he does not distinguish between causes proximate and remote. By looking round here and there, men do not find how they can transfer the blame for their destruction, because the proximate cause resides in themselves. For if they should complain that the wound is inflicted on them from another quarter, the internal sense of their mind will hold them bound to the conclusion that evil arose from the voluntary defection of the first man. I know the insolence of the carnal mind cannot be prevented from immediately protesting:[2] If God foreknew the fall of Adam and was willing to apply no remedy, we innocently perish from His eternal decree rather than render the just penalty of sin. And, supposing no such thing to be foreseen by God, none the less the same complaint against original sin remains. For impiety will object to God: Why did not Adam sin in solitude so as alone to bear the penalty? why did he involve us unmerited in participation in the same disaster? indeed by what right does God transfer to us the penalty of another's fault? But when all

---

[1] French omits this.   [2] French adds: for this blasphemy is very common.

has been said, the internal feeling of the heart does not cease
to urge on everyone the conviction that no one, even being his
own judge, may be absolved. Nor truly can anyone contend
against this. For as on account of the sin of one man a lethal
wound was inflicted on all, so all men acknowledge God's
judgment to be just. We cannot avoid concluding that the first
origin of ruin is in Adam and that we individually find the
proximate cause in ourselves. What can then prevent our faith
adoring from afar with due humility the hidden counsel of God
by which the fall of man was foreordained, and yet acknowledging what appears to be our own part, that the whole human
race in the person of Adam is bound to the penalty of eternal
death and therefore subject to death? Therefore Pighius has
not shattered, as he thought, the splendid and fitting symmetry
in which the causes proximate and remote agree with one
another.

Readers must be warned that Pighius condemns equally two
propositions: that God from the beginning, when the state of
man was still intact, decreed what would be his future; and
that He now elects from the mass of perdition whom He wills.
He ridicules Augustine and those like him, that is all the godly,
for imagining that, after He had foreseen the universal ruin[1] of
the human race in the person of Adam, God destined some to
life and others to destruction. For since he takes it as agreed
that the counsel of God concerning the creation of all men to
salvation was antecedent to the fall of Adam, he does not doubt
that this purpose remains fixed to this end. For otherwise God
would not be consistent with Himself and His immutable
purpose would be subverted by man's sin. He attacks this
appearance of contradiction (as he calls it) in our doctrine. As
God decreed in Himself before the creation of Adam what
should happen to him and to his posterity, the destruction of
the reprobate ought not now to be imputed to sin; because it
would be absurd to make the effect antecedent to the cause.
But I affirm both these propositions which Pighius disputes to
be the truth. For what he holds out as disagreement between
the two propositions is none at all. We say that man was
created in such a condition that he is unable to complain to his
creator. God foresaw the fall of Adam; He did not suffer him
to fall but by His will. What place is there here for vacillation?

[1] French has: the ruin of Adam.

Yet Pighius denies it, because the preconceived counsel concerning the salvation of all stands firm. As if there were no ready solution. Salvation was offered to all on the condition that they persisted in original innocence. For no sane person will allow that the decree of God that all should come to salvation was simple and absolute. For when placed in the way of salvation, it was sufficient for man's just condemnation that he voluntarily fell from it. But it could not be otherwise. What then? is he freed from a fault which lay wholly within his will? If Augustine had said that it was once purposed by God to save all, Pighius' argument might have had some validity in refuting his opinion. But when he records that Adam on being first created was so constituted the heir of life that his own abdication was not at all hidden from God and indeed was as it were included in His secret counsel, Augustine rightly and truly infers that the reprobate are so held and bound in universal guilt that, being left in death, they suffer a just judgment. I hold the same thing. As in Adam we are all to a man lost, those who perish, perish by God's just judgment; and at the same time I declare that anything that befell Adam was ordained by God.

VIII. REFUTATION OF PIGHIUS

VIII.1. Preaching

Now I want to consider not so much what and how Pighius speaks, as how this worthless fellow may fall and lie buried under the ruins of his desperate impudence. So pious consciences will be reassured; for, as I know, they are often disturbed because of their inexperience. So I shall select from the almost unlimited stream of his loquacity whatever is specious, so that all may perceive that with all his speaking he says nothing.[1] That Christ, the redeemer of the whole world, commands the Gospel to be preached promiscuously to all does not seem congruent with special election. But the Gospel is an embassy of peace by which the world is reconciled to God, as Paul teaches (II Cor 5.18); and on the same authority it is announced that those who hear are saved. I answer briefly that Christ was so ordained for the salvation of the whole world that He might save those who are given to Him by the Father, that

[1] French has: I shall then repeat summarily the arguments which give such support to Satan, and shall show that they are only smoke.

He might be their life whose head He is, and that He might receive those into participation of His benefits whom God by His gratuitous good pleasure adopted as heirs for Himself. Which of these things can be denied? So the apostle pronounces the prophecy of Isaiah to be fulfilled in Him: Behold, I and the children whom the Lord gave me (Is 8.18; Heb 2.13). Christ Himself declares: All that the Father gave Me, I keep lest any perish (Jn 6.37). We read everywhere that He diffuses life only to members of His. And whoever will not allow that to be grafted into His body is a special gift has never read attentively the Epistle to the Ephesians. From this follows also a third thing: the virtue of Christ belongs only to the sons of God. Even those opposed to me will concede that the universality of the grace of Christ is not better judged than from the preaching of the Gospel. But the solution of the difficulty lies in seeing how the doctrine of the Gospel offers salvation to all. That it is salvific for all I do not deny. But the question is whether the Lord in His counsel here destines salvation equally for all. All are equally called to penitence and faith; the same mediator is set forth for all to reconcile them to the Father—so much is evident. But it is equally evident that nothing can be perceived except by faith, that Paul's word should be fulfilled: the Gospel is the power of God for salvation to all that believe (Rom 1.16). But what can it be for others but a savour of death to death? as he elsewhere says (II Cor 2.16).

Further, since it is clear that out of the many whom God calls by His external voice very few believe, if I prove that the greater part remain unbelieving because God honours with illumination none but those whom He will, then I draw another conclusion. The mercy of God is offered equally to both kinds of men, so that those who are not inwardly taught are rendered only inexcusable. Some make a distinction here, that the Gospel has the power to save all, but not the effect. But this does not at all dispose of the difficulty, for we are always forced back on the question whether an equal power to believe is conferred on all. But Paul gives the reason why all do not obey the Gospel; for Isaiah says: Lord who has believed our report and to whom is the arm of the Lord revealed? (Rom 10.16; Is 53.1). The prophet, astounded at the small number of believers, exclaims that it is quite unworthy that, while the word of God sounds in the ears of all, it should inwardly affect hardly any hearts. But lest so great a depravity in the world should disturb anyone, he immediately adds that this is not given to all. In a word, Paul indicates that all clamorous sounding of the human voice will lack effect, unless the virtue of God works internally in the heart. Luke puts an outstanding testimony of this before us when, having recorded the sermon preached by Paul, he says that as many as were ordained to eternal life believed (Acts 13.48). Why was the same doctrine not received by the minds of all? Luke draws the line of definition: Because not all were ordained to life. Whence comes this disposition, but of God alone? Those who suggest that they were ordained by the motion of their own hearts deserve no more refutation than those who say the world was created by itself. For it lies in the hidden wisdom of the Gospel which human ingenuity is unable to penetrate. The natural man, says Paul, does not receive the things of God (I Cor 2.14). Because he does not will so? This is indeed true: all are rebels who are not tamed by His Spirit. But Paul carries the matter to a higher level. There is such foolishness in man that he is unable to understand; no one has been God's counsellor, nor are His secrets to be known except by His Spirit alone. Hence he concludes that those only are true disciples of God who are granted the spirit not of the world but of heaven, that they may know the things given them by God. What is intended by the comparison between the spirit of the world and the Spirit of God? Just this, that men subsisting on the earth are wise in their own way only, while the heavenly Father illumines His sons specially. Here Pighius obtrudes upon us the voluntary preparation of each, if God please. As if Paul did not address himself to the Corinthians, and a little later describe them as having been thieves, drunkards, slanderers, dissolute, and infected with prodigious crimes, until they were cleansed by the sanctification of the Spirit (I Cor 6.9). What quality for meeting the illumination proffered to them could they have whom God drew out of hell itself? And what need is there of proceeding in a great circle of words? The Spirit who reveals to us the secrets of the kingdom of heaven is the Spirit of adoption. But adoption is gratuitous. Hence the Spirit Himself is bestowed gratuitously. Now experience teaches that the Spirit is not bestowed on all. Hence faith is a special gift by which the election of God is ratified. Paul in this sense speaks of

Christ, to the Jews a scandal, and to the Gentiles foolishness, but to the called the power and wisdom of God (I Cor 1.23). But from where does calling come but from God who calls according to His purpose those whom He elects (Rom 8.30)? Now we hold that the Gospel which ought to be by its nature an odour of life to life is an odour of death to those who perish and who thus remain unbelieving in their darkness because the arm of God is not revealed to them. But if in such a corruption and depravity of our nature there are yet some who believe the Gospel, it is sacrilegious to ascribe it to their goodness. Rather let thanks be always rendered to God, as Paul advises, who has chosen them from the beginning of the world to salvation in sanctification of the Spirit and belief in the truth (II Thes 2.13). Certainly in these words he derives both faith and sanctification from eternal election, like two streams from one source. What then? Were these chosen because they had sanctified themselves? But Paul expressly asserts that this is the work of the Spirit of God. Since the nature of faith is the same, it remains to conclude that illumination into faith is in order that election may be ratified and manifested in its effect. And certainly when we hear that no one comes to Christ unless the Father draw him, we may accept what Augustine says:[1] Who is drawn if already willing? Yet no one comes unless he will. Hence in wonderful ways men are drawn so that they will by Him who knows how to work inwardly on the hearts of men, not that they may unwillingly believe, which is impossible, but that from being unwilling they be made willing.

VIII.2. God's will that all be saved

All this Pighius contradicts, adducing the opinion of Paul (I Tim 2.4): God wills all to be saved. That He does not will the death of a sinner is to be believed on His own oath where He says by the prophet: As I live, I do not will the death of a sinner, but rather that he may be converted and live (Ezek 18.23, 33.11). But I contend that, as the prophet is exhorting to penitence, it is no wonder that he pronounces God willing that all be saved. But[2] the mutual relation between threats and promises shows such forms of speech to be conditional. To the Ninevites, as also to the kings of Gerar and Egypt, God de-

---

[1] *Ad Bonif.*, lib. 1, cap. 19.
[2] Beza and Amst. have the bad reading: If.

clared that He would do what He was not going to do.[1] Since by repentance they averted the punishment promised to them, it is evident that it was not firmly decreed unless they remained obstinate. Yet the denunciation had been positive, as if it were an irrevocable decree. But after terrifying and humbling them with the sense of His wrath, though not to the point of despair, He cheers them with the hope of pardon, that they might feel there was room for remedy. So again with the promises which invite all men to salvation. They do not simply and positively declare what God has decreed in His secret counsel but what He is prepared to do for all who are brought to faith and repentance. But, it is alleged, we thereby ascribe a double will to God, whereas He is not variable and not the least shadow of turning falls upon Him. What is this, says Pighius, but to mock men, if God professes to will what He does not will? But if in fairness the two are read together: I will that the sinner turn and live, the calumny is dissolved without bother. God demands conversion from us; wherever He finds it, a man is not disappointed of the promised reward of life. Hence God is said to will life, as also repentance. But the latter He wills, because He invites all to it by His word. Now this is not contradictory of His secret counsel, by which He determined to convert none but His elect. He cannot rightly on this account be thought variable, because as lawgiver He illuminates all with the external doctrine of life, in this first sense calling all men to life. But in the other sense, He brings to life whom He will, as Father regenerating by the Spirit only His sons.

It is indeed certain that men are not converted to the Lord of their own accord; nor is the gift of conversion common to all. For this is one of the two heads of the covenant, which God promises to make with none but His children and His elect people: He will write His laws on their hearts. For it is madness for anyone to say that this is promised to all in general: I will make a covenant with them, not like that I made with their fathers; but I will write My laws on their hearts (Jer 31.33). To restrict this to those who are worthy or who have rightly prepared themselves by their own endeavour would be worse than gross folly; for the Lord addresses those whose hearts were formerly stony, as is clear from another prophet (Ezek 36.26).

[1] French has: what He has determined to do.

I admit that contumacy is common to all, nor is the heart of any flexible and obedient to God until He gives what He commands. For why are we called new creatures, unless because we are remade of God, created to every good work (Eph 2.10; II Cor 5.17)? I pray you, what kind of a partition it would be, and how unequal, if God created us mortal men, but each were his own creator to righteousness and heavenly life! For in this way God would only have for Himself the praise of fallible grace,[1] since what is much more excellent would fall to us. But Scripture affirms that to circumcise men's hearts is the work of God (Deut 30.6); nor is regeneration ascribed to any other. Hence also whatever in man is made new in the image of God is always called Spirit. The Lord does indeed frequently exhort us to repentance, but He Himself is asserted to be the author of conversion (II Tim 2.25). His law is said to convert souls (Ps 19.8ff.), and this office is elsewhere transferred to the ministers of the word (Lk 1.17). But while they labour by praying, sowing and watering, it is God alone that gives the increase (I Cor 3.6). So it is no wonder that it is ascribed to Him to open the heart of His own (Acts 16.14), so that they may attend to the word they hear. Hence Augustine[2], having treated of the elect, and taught that their salvation reposes in the faithful custody of God so that none perishes, continues: The rest of mortal men who are not of this number, but rather taken out of the common mass and made vessels of wrath, are born for the use of the elect. For God created no one of them casually or fortuitously, nor is He ignorant of whatever good may be worked through them. For that He created human nature in them and adorned the order of this present life by them is in itself a good work. But He brings none of them to the spiritual repentance by which a man is reconciled with God. Hence, though these are born of the same mass of perdition, yet according to the hardness and impenitence of their heart they all, as far as in them lies, treasure up for themselves wrath to the day of wrath. God by the goodness of His mercy brings some from the same mass of repentance, and by just judgment does not bring others. So Augustine. And lest anyone should imagine that here divine grace and our industry conflict, what he records elsewhere is always recurring. Men labour, he

---

[1] French has: of this corruptible and fallible life.
[2] *Contra Iulian.*, lib. 5, cap. 3.

says,[1] to find in our own free will what good thing we may call our own which is not from God; but I do not know anything that can be found. And a little later: Therefore not only the power of will which is free to turn this way and that and is among the natural goods which a bad man may badly use, but also the good will which is among those goods of which a bad use cannot be made, are both ours only by the gift of God. Unless we hold this, I do not know how what Paul says can be defended: What have you that you did not receive? (I Cor 4.7). But if there be in us a certain free will which is of God which may be good or evil, and a good will which is of ourselves, what proceeds from us is better than what comes from God. In the end he concludes: Where the Lord wills to bestow this gift, it is of His mercy, not of their merit; where He does not so will, it is of His truth;[2] for power to draw He certainly has.

The difficulty of another place (I Tim 2.4) is readily solved. Paul tells us that God wills all men to be saved, and also how He wills them to come to the knowledge of His truth. For he joins both together. Now I ask: Did the will of God remain the same from the beginning of the world? For if He willed that His truth be known to all, why did He not proclaim His law also to the Gentiles? Why did He confine the light of life within the narrow limits of Judaea? What does Moses mean when he says (Deut 4.8): There is no nation which has statutes and laws by which to be ruled like this people, unless to praise the privilege of the race of Abraham? To this corresponds the enconium of David (Ps 147.20): He dealt so with no other people, nor manifested His judgments to them. Nor must we overlook the express reason: Because God loved the fathers, He chose their sons; not because they were more excellent, but because it seemed good to the Lord to choose them for His peculiar people (Deut 4.37, 7.8). What then? Did Paul not know that he was prohibited by the Spirit from preaching the word of Christ in Asia and from crossing over into Bithynia where he was proceeding? (Acts 16.6). But as a full treatment of this matter would be too prolix, I content myself with one word more. When He had lit the light of life for the Jews alone, God allowed the Gentiles to wander for many ages in darkness (Acts 14.16). Then this special gift was promised to the Church, that the Lord should rise upon it and His glory be

---

[1] *De Peccat. Merit. et Remiss.*, lib. 2, cap. 18.   [2] French has: of His justice.

conspicuous in it (Is 60.2). Now let Pighius asseverate that God wills all to be saved, when not even the external preaching of the doctrine, which is much inferior to the illumination of the Spirit, is made common to all. That passage was long ago brought up by the Pelagians. What Augustine in many places replied, I refrain from stating at present, except one passage in which he shows clearly and briefly how unconcernedly he scorns the objection. When, he says,[1] our Lord complains that, for all His willingness to gather the children of Jerusalem, they would not have it, was the will of God overpowered by weak men, so that the Almighty was unable to do what He willed? Where then will be that omnipotence by which He did whatsoever pleased Him in heaven and on earth? Who will be so impiously foolish as to say that God cannot convert to good the evil wills of men when and where and in whatever cases He will? But when He does so, He does it in mercy, and when not, in judgment. But the difficulty is, I admit, not yet solved. Yet I have extorted this from Pighius, that no one unless deprived of sense and judgment can believe that salvation is ordained in the secret counsel of God equally for all. For the rest, the meaning of Paul is quite simple and clear to anyone not bent on contention. He bids solemn prayers be made for kings and princes in authority. Because in that age there were so many dangerous enemies of the Church, to prevent despair from hindering application to prayer, Paul anticipates their difficulties, declaring that God wills all men to be saved. Who does not see that the reference is to orders of men rather than individual men? Nor indeed does the distinction lack substantial ground: what is meant is not individuals of nations but nations of individuals.[2] At any rate, the context makes it clear that no other will of God is intended than that which appears in the external preaching of the Gospel. Thus Paul means that God wills the salvation of all whom He mercifully invites by preaching to Christ.[3]

---

[1] *Enchir. ad Laur.*, cap. 97 seq.

[2] The sentence is wanting in the French.

[3] French adds: If anyone retorts to the contrary, he must admit that God does not come to the end He desires or that all are saved without exception. To say that God wills what is in Himself, and at the same time leaves each man his free-will, is nonsense. For I ask once more why then He willed that the Gospel be preached from the beginning of the world to all nations. All amenable men will hold the exposition which I have given: God wills to make princes and magistrates participants of salvation as well as others.

VIII.3. Respect of persons

But Pighius renews the battle with me over respect of persons.[1] Because God is no respecter of persons,[2] he infers that all are equally loved by Him. But I answered him earlier.[3] By the term person, Scripture means all external attributes of men, which they cannot cause, but which procure favour for some and load others with hatred or contempt. Pighius thunders that nothing more inept could be said or thought. But if the matter were put to the vote, I should have many irreproachable masters and companions. One ground will suffice. In Hebrew there is a word *panim* which is equivalent to *facies* or appearance. The word is used when judges are forbidden to respect persons, when Moses testifies that God is no respecter of persons (Deut 1.17, 10.17), and also in the story of Job (32.21, 34.19). Now I ask what can we understand by the term but all kinds of external appearances, as they are commonly called, by which we are led away from the thing itself? Similarly, the apostles, when speaking of servants and masters, of Jews and Gentiles, and of the prominent and the obscure (Rom 2.11; Gal 2.6; Eph 6.9; Col 3.25), use πρόσωπον; since some have excellence more than others, and so it comes about that what is equal and just is not discerned. So Christ opposes ὄψιν, that is aspect, to just judgment (Jn 7.24), as if to say that, where the favour or hatred of men rules, it can only be that all equity and rectitude is perverted. Everyone[4] must therefore see that Pighius is carried away by rabid and petulant hatred of the truth and does not mind what he says. Now let this fine censor's amendment be heard. He declares respect of persons to be a vice that has a place in the administration of justice. From this he infers that God is no respecter of persons because He is indifferent to all, and, as befits a just distributor of public grants, shows Himself similarly liberal and beneficent. But really he gabbles, as if extinguishing the light of Scripture

---

[1] Lib. 7, cap. 2.   [2] French has: judges without regard to person.

[3] In the French this is rendered: Now it is to be noted that this word person means in Scripture aspect or face, or, better expressed, what we commonly call appearance. Thus this word means all necessary considerations which turn us from the truth of the case. Christ, however, opposes, etc. (all the rest omitted).

[4] Everyone . . . subjected to contempt—for this, the French has more briefly: Pighius says that God does not at all accept persons, and so conducts Himself indifferently to all, showing Himself liberal like a good trustee charged with distributing a public fund.

gave him the right to make things up out of his own head. For all passages in Scripture support my view, while he brings none to support his construction. And what wonder, if thereby he can safely proffer his deliriums, without even considering the meaning of the term about which he talks? He pours out words without sense and in contempt of grammar, presumably to show himself a great theologian. For person means for him nothing but man. But it is more than evident that it means an extrinsic quality in which men are clad and for which they are held in favour or subjected to contempt. But whether God is an equal dispenser or not, Christ is rather to be believed than Pighius. Now Christ introduces God in the person of father of a family, saying (Mt 20.15): Is it not lawful to do what I will with My own? is your eye evil because Mine is benign? Paul follows this reasoning to show that God is restricted by no one from dispensing His grace according to His will to whom it seems good, when he enquires: Who first gave to Him that it should be returned to him again? (Rom 11.35).

In the first place, if there had been a grain of piety in this man, could he ever have dared so insultingly to call God to order? For he prescribes that God should bestow His bounty on all, as from a public treasury.[1] Thus he leaves God nothing in which to exercise gratuitious beneficence. God, he says, judges of every individual according to his dignity and works, not according to His own good pleasure. What merit, then, moved Him to choose the race of Abraham? What dignity did He find in this race to prefer it to others? God assigns no other reason than that He loved their fathers. And more expressly: Behold, the heavens and the earth are the Lord's; yet the Lord delighted in your fathers to love them, and chose their seed after them (Deut 4.37, 10.15). In another place, He reduces all their merits to nothing, declaring them to have been idolators (Josh 24.2). At any rate, I conclude, though Pighius denies it, that the good pleasure of God is clearly preached by Moses. It is not, he says,[2] on the decree of God that the election of one and the rejection of another depend, but on the affection of men. What then does this mean: Not of works, but of Him that calls is this said, The elder shall serve the younger (Rom

---

[1] French has: as if He were a public receiver.

[2] French has: And it is remarkable how the enemies of the election of God dare to place the foundation of salvation in the good affections of men, in view of the express statement: It is not of works but of God who calls.

9.11)? The blasphemy Pighius later emits is execrable: God is made not only unjust but cruel, if He devote anyone at all to destruction. But he will one day stand before the tribunal of God who, Paul asserts, manifests His power in the vessels of wrath. Even now, lying under the shadow of his evil end, he thinks that God is not a human fabrication but always the eternal judge of the whole world. This wretched man even now experiences the truth: God triumphs when He is judged (Ps 51.6; Rom 3.4). But I admit that a godly and upright life is sometimes contrasted with person, as when Peter says that God is no προσωπολήμπτης, since in every nation whoever lives well is acceptable to Him (Acts 10.34). But the reply is immediate, that God offers the gifts He confers on His children, but in the nature of man finds nothing but what merits hatred. Hence, that God may love His worshippers, He must prevent them with His gratuitous love while unworthy and as yet devoid of all good, and give to them what afterwards He may follow up with His love. This first grace He gives to whom He will, says Augustine,[1] because He is merciful. Even if He should not give it, He is just. And He does not give it where He does not will, in order to make known the riches of His glory on the vessels of mercy. But that there is with Him no respect of persons is shown at the end of the chapter to mean that sometimes He may pass over the children of His worshippers and deliver from destruction the offspring born of the reprobate. Further, what Augustine adds is well worth remembering,[2] that no more splendid mirror of predestination exists than the mediator Himself, who according to His human nature attained without merit such honour as to be the only begotten Son of God. But[3] this good pleasure of God which He puts before us in Christ the head of the Church for contemplation, Pighius will not suffer or allow even in the members. For he contends that the blessed mother of Christ was elected on merit, for she sings: He respected the lowliness of His handmaiden (Lk 1.48). Such are Pighius' proofs for the election of God being founded on men's merits, not on grace, because He chose what was abject and contemptible.[4]

---

[1] *De Dono Persever.*, cap. 12.   [2] Ibid., cap. 24.

[3] But . . . contemptible—French has: Now if we see in the head such an example of this good pleasure of God, this is good reason for acknowledging it in the members.

[4] Lib. 8, cap. 2.

VIII.4. *The reason for election*

This reason disposes easily of another of Pighius' objections. When, he says, Christ calls the blessed of His Father to the possession of the kingdom, He does not simply state their election to be the cause, but the fact that they have done the works of charity.[1] But I do not merely send men off to the secret election of God to await with gaping mouth salvation there. I bid them make their way directly to Christ in whom salvation is offered us, which otherwise would have lain hid in God. For whoever does not walk in the plain path of faith can make nothing of the election of God but a labyrinth of destruction. Therefore, that the remission of sins may be a certainty to us, our consciences rest in confidence of eternal life, and we call upon God as Father without fear, the beginning is not to be made here. We must begin with what is revealed in Christ concerning the love of the Father for us and what Christ Himself daily preaches to us through the Gospel. Nothing higher is demanded of us than that we be the sons of God. But of the gratuitous election by which alone we may attain this highest good, the mirror, earnest and pledge is the Son, who came forth for us from the bosom of the Father to make us heirs of the heavenly kingdom by ingrafting us into His body. Further, as this inheritance was once obtained for us by the blood of Christ and is attested in the sacred pages of the Gospel, so possession of it is entered into not otherwise than by faith. In a word, I not only freely confess but emphasise everywhere in my writings both that the salvation of men is bound to faith, and that Christ is the only door by which all must enter into the heavenly kingdom; nor is tranquil peace to be found elsewhere than in the Gospel. Those who deviate in the slightest degree from this can do nothing but wander through tortuous ambiguities. The more anyone tries to invade and penetrate those profound recesses of the divine counsel, the further he recedes from God. Hence, I do not deny that the way is to be walked by faith. Hence, another matter also is disposed of. Pighius alleges that God will on the last day crown the gifts of the Spirit which He has bestowed on the elect in the present life. But this does not prevent the heavenly Father by faith and the sanctification of the Spirit engrafting those who are

[1] French adds: as is recorded in St Matthew (25.42ff.).

elect in Christ into His body, or calling and justifying in His own time those who were predestined before the foundation of the world. Paul joins both admirably when he says that all things work together for good to those who love God and immediately adds: who are called according to the purpose (Rom 8.28). This then is the way in which God governs His own; this is the manner in which He discharges His work of grace in them. But why He takes them by the hand has another superior cause, that eternal purpose, namely, by which He destined them to life. Hence the impudence of Pighius is even more ridiculous; for he does not hesitate insolently to fit to his own use a testimony directly against him. In the first place he reminds[1] us to note well that all things are not said to work for good to the elect or the loved; a different cause is rather assigned, that they love God.[2] As if indeed Paul had not paid attention to this and added the correction, lest any of the faithful should attribute to his own merit the fact that God turns all things to good for them. Paul first shows how it befits the faithful to be disposed to Him; and this is the result of their being called.[3] But lest they should cleave to themselves, he teaches that the beginnings of salvation and all blessings have a higher source, that they had first been called. This knot, too, Pighius unlooses with a jest. God, he says, calls all men to holiness.[4] As if calling were not clearly commended as efficacious in the express purpose of God. What are the deceptions by which he spreads so dense a darkness that the lucidity of the sentiment is obscured? God chose those whom He justified that He might at length glorify them (Rom 8.30)—however he may mangle this sentence, he can never stretch its efficacy to cover all men.[5] Hence it is evident what a foolish argument it is that strives to subvert election by substituting faith and works. This is to make the daughter devour the mother, as the common saying goes. There[6] is a last refuge for Pighius. God predestined none to salvation but those whom He foreknew.

[1] Lib. 8, cap. 2, end.

[2] French adds: and pretending by this that St Paul finds the cause of our salvation in us.

[3] French has: the fruits of vocation.

[4] French adds: But it is a great mockery to think that this word of purpose means an efficacy and effect of the grace of the Holy Spirit by which God accomplishes His counsel. Once again, how such calumniators dim the eyes of everyone, etc.

[5] French adds: It follows then that St Paul denotes a certain number of called.

[6] French omits what here follows to the end of the paragraph.

But this way I have already blocked against him; for I have shown it to be impossible that God should foresee anything in man that was not worthy of destruction, until He should Himself have created him anew by His Spirit. If then no one has anything which he did not receive, what more can one bring before God than another to excel him? God therefore knew His own, not estimating them by merit, but in distinguishing none from others except by casting merciful and propitious eyes on them, so as to number undeservedly whom He will among His children. As Paul has it: Who makes you different (I Cor 4.7)? But Pighius' gratuitous foreknowledge which he calls naked or without preference, is no foreknowledge at all. With what feathers, then, will he adorn man, lest he come before God naked and deformed in every part? For Scripture insists that everything in the deformed nature of man is hateful to God, and that only His own image, which is created anew in Christ, pleases Him.

Pighius continues: When we enquire the reason why the ungodly are condemned,[1] it is not this tyrannical voice with which we are met, that they were distinguished from the elect by the counsel of God, because it pleased God to devote them to destruction; as though to say: I will it so, I require it so, let my will be the reason and make it so.[2] Rather they hear the voice of Christ: I was hungry, and you gave Me food, etc. (Mt 25.42). Not very unlike this is what he repeats in another place.[3] Christ will not say to them that they are damned because they are born of the corrupt seed of Adam, because they contracted the desert of eternal death from his[4] sin, because they must perish for his fault. He will say it is because they did not give food to the starving and did not perform other works of charity. If original guilt is for Pighius not sufficient to condemn men and the hidden judgment of God has no kind of place, what will he make of those infant children who are taken from this life before they could display any such example because of their age? The infants of Sodom and of Jerusalem had the same condition of birth and death, nor was there any disparity in their works. Why then will Christ on the last day separate them

[1] French has: sent to eternal fire.
[2] French omits this well-known verse of the poet.
[3] French has: He goes even further to disgorge this blasphemy.
[4] French has: of a man.

to stand some on His right and the others on His left? Who does not here adore the admirable judgment of God by which it is ordained that some are born in Jerusalem and pass thence to a better life, while Sodom, the forecourt of hell, receives the birth of others? But as Christ awards to the elect the recompense of justice, so the reprobate will receive not less fittingly the punishment of their impiety and crimes. Nothing in my teaching goes to show that God by His eternal counsel does not elect to life those whom He pleases and leaves others to destruction; or to deny that there are punishments ordained for evil works and a prize laid up for good. We shall all stand before the tribunal of Christ, so that each may receive as he conducted himself in the body, whether good or evil. But whence come the justice and sanctity with which the pious will then be crowned, unless that God regenerated them to newness of life by His Spirit? And whence the gift of regeneration, except from gratuitous adoption? Pighius argues like a man denying that the day is created by God out of light because it is made by the splendour of the sun. This comparison is, however, not exact in every point. For the light created in the beginning has properly God for its author. But the fault of our damnation resides so entirely in ourselves that it is forbidden to assemble extraneous pretexts with which to cover it. But it was permissible thus briefly to show how preposterously Pighius removes the remote cause by bringing forward the proximate. He contends that the impious will be damned because they have provoked the wrath of God on themselves by their own misdeeds. From this he concludes that their damnation does not proceed from the decree of God. But I say they have accumulated misdeeds upon misdeeds because, being depraved, they could do nothing but sin. Yet they sinned not by extrinsic impulse but by the spontaneous inclination of the heart, knowingly and voluntarily. For it cannot be denied that the fount and origin of all evils is the corruption and viciousness of nature without overturning the first rudiments of piety. If you ask the reason why God corrects the vice in His elect but deems the reprobate unworthy of the same remedy, it is hidden in Himself. In this way Paul in the ninth chapter of the Epistle to the Romans first establishes God as the arbiter of life and death so as finally to save those whom He rescues from destruction. He then plainly pronounces that it is not of him that wills or of him that runs, but of the mercy of God who has mercy on whom He will have mercy and who hardens whom He will. After this, he shows clear and as it were palpable causes for the blindness in his own people, that the majority rejected Christ and obstinately resisted God who stretched out His hand towards them. Hence these two principles agree splendidly with each other: each man by his own unbelief is the author of his condemnation, and all destitute of the Spirit of God rush blindly against Christ. Therefore, Paul presents the Jews as guilty because, wishing to establish their own righteousness, they were not subject to the righteousness of God (Rom 10.3), and so by the vice of their pride were cast out of the Church; but at the same time it is to be ascribed to the grace of God that a certain remnant stands. So by His own declaration God maintains: There yet remain to Me seven thousand men who have not bent the knee before Baal (I Kings 19.18). Nor, as Augustine circumspectly observes,[1] did these stand by their own virtue; for the Lord saved them to constitute a remnant. Paul is even more explicit: The remnant gathered by the coming of Christ is saved according to gratuitous election (Rom 11.5). You note the term remnant. It signifies a small number separated from the general mass of mankind. He says these were saved not for their own virtue, but by the goodness of God. He derived salvation from gratuitous election, meaning that this was the sole cause why they did not perish in the general mass, because they were gratuitously elected. From this it follows that if all were elect none would perish.

If a mortal man should pronounce his will and command and make his volition a sufficient reason, I admit it would be tyrannical. But to transfer[2] the principle to God would be sacrilegious folly. For no immoderation may be attributed to God, as if desire surged in Him as in men. Rather such honour is rightly ascribed to His will that it constitutes a sufficient reason, since it is the origin and rule of all righteousness. For the distinction commonly made in the schools of a twofold will we by no means admit. The sophists of the Sorbonne talk of a regulative and an absolute will of God. This blasphemy is rightly abhorrent to pious ears but is plausible to Pighius and those like him. But I contend on the contrary that, so far from there being anything unordained in God, rather all order

[1] *De Dono Persever.*, cap. 18.   [2] French has: to fit God to such a measure.

traceable in heaven or earth originates in Him.[1] When therefore, we carry the will of God to the highest level so as to be
higher than all reason, we do not at all imagine that He does
anything but with the highest reason. Our view is simply that
He possesses by right such great power, that we ought to be
content with His mere nod. For if it is truly said: Thy judgments
are a great deep (Ps 36.7), when the mind of man thrusts
forward to such lengths in its pride as not to rest simply in the
good pleasure of God, let it be warned lest such a great deep
swallow him up. It cannot well be otherwise; and this vengeance is more than just. Hence Augustine's word[2] should never
be forgotten: Attend to who God is and who you are. He is
God, you are man. Should you think you are talking of justice,
is the fount of justice dried up? You as a man expect an answer
from me. But I also am a man. Let us both therefore listen to
one who speaks: O man, who art thou? Better is the ignorance
of faith than the temerity of knowledge! Seek for merit, and
you will find only punishment. O the height and the depth!
Peter denies, the thief believes. O the height and the depth!
You ask a reason. I stand in awe before the height and the
depth. You ratiocinate, I admire; you dispute, I believe. I see
the height, but I do not comprehend the depth. Paul rests
quietly because he found wonder. He calls the judgments of
God inscrutable—do you mean to scrutinise them? He says His
ways are past finding out—do you propose to find them out?
Similarly in another place[3] he says: Will you dispute with me?
Rather admire with me and exclaim: O the height and the
depth! Let us agree to tremble together lest together we perish
in error.

To himself, Pighius seems to argue acutely when he denies
that the judgments of God would be a great deep, if His will
were the highest reason; for nothing would be easier than that
all things be made because God so pleased, where His will alone
ruled. But this garrulous sophistry foolishly overlooks the issue
at stake. All things are rightly done because God pleased; but
why did He please so and not otherwise? He proceeds with his
inept argument; and, to show that God had a cause within His
own counsels, he adduces the reply Christ gave to His disciples,
that the man was born blind that the works of God might be

---

1 French adds: as ordaining well and fitly all that is in nature.
2 *De Verbis Apost.*, serm. 20.   3 *De Verbis Apost.*, serm. 11.

manifested in him (Jn 9.3). It is Pighius' custom[1] to arrange a
shadow fight. But where was it suggested by me that God's
counsel had no reason? I establish God as ruler of the whole
world, who governs and moderates all things by incomprehensible and admirable counsel. Can anyone gather from my
words that God is carried hither and thither fortuitously or
that He does what He does in blind temerity? Indeed a little
later Pighius quotes words of mine, which unless I am mistaken,
are plainly sufficient to refute him. I say[2] that God has a purpose in His works, however hidden, that He may declare the
glory of His name. In this, Pighius would show his readers an
appearance of contradiction, that I deny that the reason of the
divine good pleasure is to be sought, and yet at the same time
teach what this reason is. But it is useless to show in detail how
barren this nonsense is. In all His works, the Lord has the
reason of His own glory. This precisely is the universal end.
On the testimony of Paul (Rom 9.17), He raised up Pharaoh
that His name might be declared in all the earth. Does Paul
contradict himself when he then exclaims that His judgments
are inscrutable (Rom 11.33)? He declares that the vessels of
wrath destined to destruction are endured in great patience
that He might show His power in them (Rom 9.22); is this
opinion contradicted by the admiration which immediately
follows: O the height and depth? Add to this the deceit
Pighius contrives about the term cause, bringing in the final
in place of the formal cause. For though the end to which God
looks is not obscure, it does not forthwith appear why it pleased
Him so to do. This, then, is the core of the present matter.
Though God does not demonstrate His righteousness to us by
plain arguments, it none the less remains that whatever He
does is done in righteousness. We should therefore rest in His
will alone, so that to know it is His good pleasure, even if the
cause escape us, suffices us more than a thousand reasons.
Hence the folly of Pighius in objecting to the charge of incon-
sistency, when I deny that the reason of the divine will is to be
enquired into and yet emphasise that He wills nothing but
what He deems to be expedient. For, he says, the latter suggests
a cause which elsewhere I deny we are able to give. But what

[1] It is . . . temerity—French has: Everything reduces to this, that God does
nothing without reason.
[2] French has: in my *Institutes*.

knowledge of the cause do we suggest by saying that God does with deliberation what he does and what thus seems to Him expedient, while yet the specific and exact reason of His work and counsel escapes us? Added to this, he holds of no importance the difference between the reverence of faith and the audacity of inquisitiveness, and preposterously takes what I teach to be the content of faith for that common knowledge which humanity possesses. On this standard, anyone affirming that God has the best of reasons for acting, and afterwards exclaiming with Paul that the judgments of God are hidden and His ways incomprehensible, convicts himself of contradiction. Here, however,[1] Pighius is mistaken: for he demands that I acknowledge my own words which in fact I take from Augustine. When the question is asked, says this holy man,[2] why God acts so, the answer is: Because He willed. If you go on to enquire why He so willed, the reply should be: You ask for something greater and higher than the will of God itself, and this cannot be found. Let human temerity, then, be repressed, not asking for what is not, lest perhaps it do not find what is. Augustine here speaks the truth, and I fully subscribe to it. But the view given above contains nothing that dissents from these words: the will of God is the best and most equal adjustment of all the things He has made.

VIII.5. *The reason for reprobation*

Of the same kind of stuff is another objection. I deny that the reprobate are distinguished from the elect in respect of any merit of their own; for the grace of God makes and does not find them worthy of adoption, as Augustine often says. Elsewhere I deny that any injury is done the reprobate, for they deserve destruction. Here[3] Pighius spreads his wings and noisily exults, that in this case I neither understand myself nor remember what I previously said. But it does not seem to me worth while to say many words in my own defence, and I am displeased at having to use even a few. When God prefers some to others, choosing some and passing others by, the difference does not depend on human dignity or indignity. It is therefore

---

[1] Here, however . . . Augustine—French has: This is what St Augustine says.

[2] *De Genes. contra Manichaeos*, lib. 1, cap. 3.

[3] Here Pighius . . . even a few—French has: more simply: Pighius finds this very distasteful. But the solution is quite easy.

wrong to say that the reprobate are worthy of eternal destruction. If in the former case no comparison is made between men
themselves, and worthiness has no relation to the reward of life,
so in the second case the equal condition of all is not proved.
Add to this that Augustine writes in one place that salvation
never lacked to anyone worthy of it, but qualifies the statement
in the *Retractations*[1] so as to exclude works and to refer acceptable worthiness to the gratuitous calling of God. But Pighius
presses on. If what I teach is true, that those who perish are
destined to death by the eternal good pleasure of God though
the reason does not appear, then they are not found but made
worthy of destruction. I reply that three things must here be
considered.

First, the eternal predestination of God, by which before the
fall of Adam He decreed what should take place concerning the
whole human race and every individual, was fixed and determined. Secondly, Adam himself, on account of his defection,
is appointed to death. Lastly, in his person now fallen and
lost, all his offspring is condemned in such a way that God
deems worthy of the honour of adoption those whom He
gratuitously elects out of it. I neither dream nor fabricate
anything of this. Nor am I called on in the present instance
to prove each particular, because I fancy I have done this
already. But I must dispose of this calumny of Pighius who
proudly triumphs over me as though I were vanquished ten
times, for the reason that these things are quite inconsistent.[2]
When predestination is discussed, it is from the start to be constantly maintained, as I today teach, that all the reprobate are
justly left in death, for in Adam they are dead and condemned.
Those justly perish who are by nature children of wrath. Thus,
no one has cause to complain of the too great severity of God,
seeing that all carry in themselves inclusive liability. As to the
first man, we must hold he was created perfectly righteous and
fell by his own will; and hence it comes about that by his own
fault he brought destruction on himself and on all his race.
Adam fell, though not without God's knowledge and ordination, and destroyed himself and his posterity;[3] yet this neither

[1] Lib. 2, cap. 31.

[2] But I must . . . inconsistent—French has: But it will be sufficient for the
moment to show that there is no contradiction in my teaching.

[3] and destroyed himself and his posterity—lacking in the French.

mitigates his guilt nor involves God in any blame. For we must always remember that he voluntarily deprived himself of the rectitude he had received from God, voluntarily gave himself to the service of sin and Satan, and voluntarily precipitated himself into destruction. One excuse is suggested, that he could not evade what God had decreed. But his voluntary transgression is enough and more than enough to establish his guilt. For the proper and genuine cause of sin is not God's hidden counsel but the evident will of man. The foolish complaint of Medea is rightly derided by the ancient poet: O that the wooden planks cut with the axes in the grove of Pelius had never fallen on the earth! She had betrayed her country, carried away by furious love of an unknown stranger. But when she awakes to her own perfidy and barbarous cruelty, when the shame of immodesty overwhelms her, she foolishly resorts to causes that are quite remote.[1] Since a man may find the cause of his evil within himself, what is the use of looking round to seek it in heaven? Clearly the fault lies in this, that she willed to sin. Why does she then break into the recesses of heaven and lose herself in such a labyrinth? Though men delude themselves by wandering through obscure immensities,[2] they can never so stupefy themselves as to lose the sense of sin engraved on their hearts. Hence, impiety attempts in vain to absolve the man whom his own conscience condemns. God knowingly and willingly suffers man to fall; the reason may be hidden, but it cannot be unjust. This is always to be held above controversy, that sin is always hateful to God. For truly the praise which David accords Him (Ps 5.5) is fitting: God wills not iniquity.[3]

[1] The allusion is to two surviving verses from the *Medea* of Ennius, also other authors, Varro, Quintilian, Priscian, frequently highly praised by Cicero (*De Fato*, 15, *De Inventione*, I, 49, *De Natura Deorum*, III, 30, *Topica.*, 16, etc.), which have come down thus:

Utinam ne in memore Pelio securibus
Caesa cecidisset abiegna ad terram trabes.

The words, however, belong not to Medea but to the nurse. The French version runs thus: He introduces the licentious daughter of a king, who, being inflamed with foolish love for a stranger who has come by sea to her father's country, betrays the kingdom to him. Then, seeing herself deceived by him, she laments that the timber of the forest was cut for building the ship. Now the poet writes wisely to show how foolish men are to seek from afar vain excuses to cover their sins. This unhappy woman is convicted by her own conscience, while demanding: Why was the timber cut to make the ship? This is to seek a too remote cause.

[2] French has: let men scurry round as they will.

[3] French adds: he attributes to Him a title inseparable from His divine essence and majesty.

So God in ordaining the fall of man had an end most just and right which holds the name of sin in abhorrence. Though I affirm that He ordained it so, I do not allow that He is properly the author of sin. Not to spend longer on the point, I am of opinion that what Augustine teaches[1] was fulfilled: In a wonderful and ineffable way, what was done contrary to His will was yet not done without His will, because it would not have been done at all unless He had allowed it. So He permitted it not unwillingly but willingly. For the principle that here operates cannot be denied: men and angels as to themselves did what God did not will, but as to the omnipotence of God they were by no means able to effect it. To this opinion of this holy man I subscribe: in sinning, they did what God did not will in order that God through their evil will might do what He willed. If anyone object that this is beyond his comprehension, I confess it. But what wonder if the immense and incomprehensible majesty of God exceed the limits of our intellect? I am so far from undertaking the explanation of this sublime, hidden secret, that I wish what I said at the beginning to be remembered, that those who seek to know more than God has revealed are crazy. Therefore let us be pleased with instructed ignorance rather than with the intemperate and inquisitive intoxication of wanting to know more than God allows. Let all the powers of the human mind contain themselves within this kind of reverence: in the sin of man God willed nothing but what was worthy of His justice.

Pighius continues: If the apostasy of man be the work of God, what Scripture says is false, that all things which God does are good. Now I must solemnly testify and frankly confess that this objection never entered my head. I always affirm that the nature of man is at first created upright, lest the depravity which he contracted should be ascribed to God; and similarly that the death to which, though formerly the heir of life, he rendered himself subject proceeded from his own fault so that God cannot be considered its author. If anywhere I have said that the first man alienated himself from God at the prompting of the divine Spirit, and did not rather always contend that it was by instigation of the devil and the motion of his own heart, Pighius might justly have attacked me. But now, removing from God all proximate causation of the act, I at the

[1] *Enchir. ad Laur.*, cap. 99.

same time remove from Him all guilt and leave man alone liable. It is therefore wicked and calumnious to say that I make the fall of man one of the works of God. But how it was ordained by the foreknowledge and decree of God what man's future was without God being implicated as associate in the fault as the author or approver of transgression, is clearly a secret so much excelling the insight of the human mind, that I am not ashamed to confess ignorance. Far be it from any of the faithful to be ashamed of ignorance of what the Lord withdraws into the glory of His inaccessible light. I prescribe nothing to others but what comes out of the experience of my heart. For the Lord is my witness, and my conscience attests it, that I daily so meditate on these mysteries of His judgments that curiosity to know anything more does not attract me; no sinister suspicion concerning His justice steals away my confidence; no desire to complain entices me. In a word, I acquiesce quietly and willingly in the opinion of Augustine:[1] God who created all things good foreknew that evil would arise out of that good; and He also knew that to make good out of evil would be more appropriate to His omnipotent goodness than not to allow evil at all. So He ordained the life of men and angels that He might first show in it what their freewill could do, and then what the blessing of His grace and the judgment of His justice could do. To these opinions I give my assent, only adding that, if the ears of any so itch that they will have none of the mysteries of God hidden and closed to them, it would be a mad master who would attempt to satisfy such pupils.[2] Rather let us hear with awe what happened to David when he enquired too narrowly into the customary[3] judgments of God as they appeared in the external circumstances and conditions of this life: I was as a beast before Thee (Ps 73.22). Even such a prophet as David cannot know more than is right of things less obscure and recondite than in the present case, without immediately being made to feel like a brute beast. Can we then with impunity indulge a foolish licence of thought in investigating the counsel of God which of all things is the most profound? When Paul taught that God chose and reprobated

---

[1] *De Correp. et Gratia*, cap. 10.

[2] French has: unless in place of being master to the curious, he should change to being prince of the desperate.

[3] So the chief MS. and Gallasius; later versions join *in* and *usitata* = uncommon; French simply omits.

out of the mass of perdition those whom He willed, he does not attempt to say why or how this happens, but rather wonderingly breaks out into exclamation: O the height and depth (Rom 11.33). Shall we, unawed by reverence for that height and depth, dare to investigate how the whole race was in the person of Adam allowed to fall? I have said above that the fall of Adam is a useful lesson in humility to his posterity, so that they may learn that they can do nothing to regain the life in which, though perfect, he did not persist. The one right rule of wisdom is for the mind of man to be restrained by the bridle of wonder.[1]

But it is right to treat this question sparingly, not because it is abstruse and hidden in the inner recesses of the sanctuary of God, but because an idle curiosity is not to be indulged; for of this, too daring speculation is both foster-child and nurse. I much approve what Augustine has to say in the *De Genesi ad Litteram*,[2] where he subjects all things to the fear and reverence of God. But the other part, showing that God chose out of the condemned race of Adam those whom He pleased and reprobated whom He willed, is much more fitting for the exercise of faith and so yields greater profit. Hence, I emphasise more willingly this doctrine which deals with the corruption and guilt of human nature, since it seems to me not only more conducive to piety but also more theological.[3] But let us remember that in these things we must reason soberly and modestly, lest we should try to go farther than the Lord leads us by His word. We know all too well the captivating allurements of argument. Hence, the greater the caution to be exercised in order that the simplicity of faith hold all our senses bound to itself. That God draws men to Himself by the secret influence of His Spirit, even our daily prayers testify. For when we pray for our persecutors, what else do we ask for them than that from being unwilling they be made willing, agreeing instead of repudiating, loving instead of opposing? But it is clear that it is not given to all indifferently that God should suddenly deem worthy of life those deserving of death a hundred times over. How He bestows this grace, says Augustine,[4]

---

[1] French adds: within the limits of this judgment of God.

[2] Lib. 11, capp. 4-8.

[3] French has: more appropriate to Christian doctrine and so more edifying.

[4] *Ad Bonif.*, lib. 1, cap. 20.

making some vessels of wrath according to merit and others vessels of mercy according to grace—who has known the mind of the Lord? Though the pride and stubbornness of the world protest against this,[1] yet it is intolerable that the condition of God be worse than that of mortal man. For what creditor is not permitted to exact debt from one and to remit it for another? This simile is often relevantly repeated by Augustine. It can hardly be but that at first glance the mind of man is disturbed when he hears that the grace of God is denied to some who are quite unworthy and is granted to others equally unworthy. But let us remember that, after we were all equally condemned, it is neither right nor just to impose a restraint on God in having mercy on whom He will. Augustine rightly contends[2] that divine justice is not to be measured by human justice. When all is said, let this conclude all disputations, as with Paul we marvel at such profundity. If impudent tongues protest,[3] let us not be ashamed or grieved to exclaim with the same apostle: O man, who art thou that contendest against God?

VIII.6. Christ's place in election

The absurdities which the adversaries of this doctrine muster in order to calumniate and defame it, I have clearly and succinctly refuted in my *Institutes*; and I fancy I have also met the distorted suppositions with which the ignorant delude and bewilder themselves. But since it pleases Pighius to nibble away at my replies, I will not decline to clear myself of his virulent charges. Men preposterously ask how they can be certain of a salvation which lies in the hidden counsel of God. I have replied with the truth. Since the certainty of salvation is set forth to us in Christ, it is wrong and injurious to Christ to pass over this proffered fountain of life from which supplies are available, and to toil to draw life out of the hidden recesses of God. Paul testifies indeed that we were chosen before the foundation of the world; but, he adds, in Christ (Eph 1.4). Let no one then seek confidence in his election elsewhere, unless he wish to obliterate his name from the book of life in which it is written. The end of adoption is simply that we should be

---

[1] French has: like escaped horses.

[2] *De Praed. et Gratia*, cap. 2 [but Augustine's authorship doubtful].

[3] French has: if false tongues should throw their poison against God.

considered His children. But Scripture declares that all those who believe in the only begotten Son of God are sons and heirs of God (Jn 1.12; Gal 4.7; Rom 8.17). Christ therefore is for us the bright mirror of the eternal and hidden election of God, and also the earnest and pledge. But we contemplate by faith the life which God represents to us in this mirror; and by faith we lay hold on this pledge and earnest. How do we prove that some men are gratuitously elect, unless because God illumines whom He will by His Spirit, so that by faith they are engrafted into the body of Christ? But divine election is the origin and cause of our faith. But because God is invisible (I Tim 1.17), and dwells in light inaccessible (I Tim 6.16), admitting none to His counsel (Rom 11.34; I Cor 2.16), except the only begotten Son who is eternally in His bosom (Jn 1.18), it is needful to hold the mind of Christ and to be illuminated by faith, in order that it may be clear to us what is the adoption that lies in the heart of God. If anyone will have it put more bluntly, election is prior to faith, but is learnt by faith. I extract briefly here what readers will find expounded at greater length in my *Institutes*.[1] Therefore Christ, when commending the eternal election of His own in the counsel of His Father, at the same time shows where their faith may rest secure. I have manifested, He says (Jn 17.6), Thy name to the men whom Thou didst give Me. Thine they were, and Thou didst give them to Me, and they have kept Thy word. We see here that God begins with Himself when He sees fit to elect us;[2] but He will have us begin with Christ so that we may know that we are reckoned among His peculiar people. For God is said to give us to the Son so that each may know himself an heir of the heavenly kingdom so long as he abides in Christ, apart from whom death and destruction beset us on every side. Christ is therefore said to manifest the name of the Father to us because by His Spirit He seals on our hearts the knowledge of our election testified to us by the voice of His Gospel.

If Pighius[3] is to be believed, the way in which I labour and toil to solve this inexplicable problem, turning everything upside down and confusing and confounding the issues, only

---

[1] This sentence is wanting in the French; in its place is inserted: For God chose and marked us before we thought of Him, before even we were born, that believing in Christ we should begin to understand election.

[2] French adds: that is, He does not seek the cause of it elsewhere.

[3] If Pighius . . . of shame—French omits.

goes to show that I am condemned by my own conscience. It was very easy for him to pour forth his loquacity without effort; and so it becomes possible for him, like a man well inebriated, to emit whatever abuse inflates his cheeks without any kind of shame. If the predestination of God is the fixed and inevitable cause of salvation, he contends that all our confidence is taken away from us. I offer no word of my own; but when Paul teaches (Eph 1.4) that we are made participants of the divine adoption by faith in that we were elected before the foundation of the world, what, I ask, is inexplicable or perplexing in this doctrine? When he teaches that those are called according to purpose who were first of all elected (Rom 8.28), unless I am mistaken, he correctly reconciles the certainty of our faith with the fixed decree of divine election.

Pighius argues:[1] If all the members of Christ are written in the book of life, then drunkards, adulterers, thieves, perjurers and murderers will possess the kingdom of God, in contradiction to the plain opinion of the apostle, who declares that many such people have been engrafted into Christ by baptism and have put on Christ. First of all, I advise my readers to pay attention for a moment to the unrestrained profanation of Scripture in which Pighius indulges, and then to observe the just judgment of God in avenging it, which he plainly exemplifies in himself.[2] To trample[3] all Scripture under his feet is nothing to Pighius, if only he can deceive his readers; and if only he can make himself look great to the inexperienced, it is all the same to him if he has to demolish the very first rudiments of piety. But the Lord exposes him in his madness to the ridicule of His children. Paul represents (Rom 2.29) circumcision as of letter and of spirit. We must think similarly of baptism. Some carry in their bodies the mere sign, but are far from possessing the reality. For Peter also, teaching that salvation follows on our baptism, immediately adds as though in correction that the mere external washing of the flesh is not enough, unless there is added also the answer of a good conscience (I Pet 3.21). Thus Scripture, in dealing with the sacraments, customarily speaks of them in a twofold sense.

---

[1] French has: Pighius has the effrontery to allege.
[2] French has: as appears in his stupidity.
[3] To trample . . . rudiments of piety—wanting in the French.

When dealing with hypocrites who glory in the sign and neglect the reality, in order to prostrate their confidence, it separates the reality from the signs, in contrast to their perverse understanding. Thus Paul (I Cor 10.3ff.) reminds his readers that it did not profit the ancient people to have been baptised in their passage through the Red Sea and to have with us the same spiritual food in the desert (meaning, that is, that they participated with us in the same external signs of the spiritual gifts).[1] But addressing the faithful he describes the use of the sacraments as legitimate, efficacious and corresponding to the divine institution.[2] It is here that the phrases apply: to have put on Christ, engrafted into His body, buried together with Him, who have been baptised in His name (Rom 6.4; Col 2.12; Gal 3.27; I Cor 12.27). From this Pighius concludes that all sprinkled with the visible element of water are truly regenerated by the Spirit and incorporated into the body of Christ so as to live to God and in His righteousness. Nor is he ashamed to fill page after page with such inanities; but when in general I refer to all the members of Christ, in this term I include all sprinkled externally in baptism.[3] But a little later,[4] as if drawing in his wings, Pighius remarks that many fall away from Christ who had been truly engrafted into His body; for he makes out that those committed to Christ and received into His faithful care are saved by Him in such a way that their salvation is dependent on their own free will. To many, he says, the protecting grace of Christ is not wanting; but they are wanting in themselves. Certainly the stupidity and ingratitude of those who withdraw themselves from the help of God can never be sufficiently condemned. But it is a quite intolerable insult to Christ to say that the elect are saved by Him, provided they look after themselves. This is to render doubtful the protection of Christ which He affirms is invincible against the devil and all the machinations of hell. Christ promised to give eternal life to all given Him by the Father (Jn 17.2). He testifies that He is a faithful custodian of them all,

---

[1] French adds: We see how he here takes the mere sign in the perverse sense of those who abuse it.

[2] French adds: and yet joins it with the virtue of the Holy Spirit.

[3] Note the meaning given by the French: he is not ashamed to fill many pages with the nonsense that all who have received the visible sign of baptism ought to be accounted members of Christ.

[4] End of lib. 7.

so that none perishes except the son of perdition (Jn 17.12). Elsewhere He also teaches that the elect are in His hand, from which no one can pluck them out (Jn 10.28), because God is mightier than all the world. If eternal life is certain to all the elect, if no one can pluck them from Him, if no violence nor any assault can tear them from Him, if their salvation stands in the invincible power of God, what impudence for Pighius to dare to shake so fixed a certitude! Though Christ casts none out, he says, yet many depart from Him, and those who once were children of God do not continue so. But Pighius is a bad and perverse interpreter, not acknowledging that whatever is given Him by the Father is retained in the hand of Christ, so that it remains safe to the end; for those that fall away, John declares to be not of His flock. They went from us, but they were not of us; for if they had been of us, they would certainly have remained with us: they went from us, that they might be made manifest that they were not all of us (I Jn 2.19).

VIII.7. *Perseverance*

Then,[1] says Pighius, the condition imposed is empty, that whoever desires to be saved should persevere up to the end. But you must allow that this is prevarication. He undertook to prove that certainty of salvation is inconsistent with election. Now his reasoning leads to the conclusion that the former is necessarily founded upon the latter. Thus I see myself perpetually tossed about, so that there is not a moment when I do not seem to be sinking. Nevertheless, as God sustains His elect to prevent them drowning, I am confident of standing against these innumerable storms.[2] If Pighius asks how I know I am elect, I answer that Christ is more than a thousand testimonies to me. For when we find ourselves in His body, our salvation rests in a secure and tranquil place, as though already located in heaven. If he objects that the eternal election of God[3] cannot be estimated by present grace, I shall not oppose to him the feelings which the faithful experience,

---

[1] French has: Our adversaries argue that if the elect thus cannot fall, the doctrine is superfluous that says: He who persists to the end shall be saved. But on the contrary, be this as it may, all of us seem to be floating on the sea, etc.

[2] French adds: Hence, His elect are encouraged to be constant by being so commanded by God.

[3] French has: what will befall tomorrow or later.

because the bread on which the children of God feed is not to be given to strangers. But[1] when he dares to allege that it is not to be found in Scripture, this is a gross falsehood easily disproved. For Paul teaches that those who were elected are called and justified, so as to attain at length to the bliss of immortality; and then, as if fortified on all sides by a powerful defence, he triumphantly exults: Who shall stand against the elect of God? etc. (Rom 8.33). And lest anyone should object that this is a universalist doctrine,[2] he applies it for the use of each believer. I am persuaded, he says, that neither death nor life, nor angels nor principalities, nor things present or future will separate us from the love of God which is in Christ. So the confidence of eternal salvation, which Pighius wants to break up into single moments, Paul extends to future time beyond the limits of this present life, and shows that it emanates from nowhere but the election of God, while Pighius represents it so that a conflict between the two results. What then does Ezekiel (18.24) mean when he pronounces destruction for the just man if he turn aside from the right way?[3] Now we do not deny that many things are found alike in the reprobate and in the children of God. But, however they shine with the appearance of righteousness, it is certain they are not possessed of the Spirit of adoption, so that their owners may truly invoke God as Father. Paul is witness that none are led by that Spirit except the sons of God, whom he also pronounces to be heirs of eternal life (Rom 8.14). Otherwise what he writes elsewhere would not stand: We have the Spirit from heaven, so that we know what things are given us by God, and thus have the mind of Christ (I Cor 2.12, 16); and in vain would he also call that Spirit with which the faithful are sealed the earnest of future redemption (Eph 1.14). But that the known election of God may strengthen the faith of perseverance, that one prayer of Christ should suffice for proof, where He commends all the elect to the Father, specifically separating them from the world, so that, even if it perish, they may remain safe and intact.

[1] French has: But those who bear the seal of the Holy Spirit imprinted on their hearts know well that the assurance of faith is not for a day, and that we have good proof of it, etc.

[2] French adds: according to which all are assured of their particular salvation.

[3] French adds: from which he concludes that the man who was once righteous may change and so fall from salvation into damnation.

VIII.8. Exhortation

There follows another objection of Pighius. Paul surely does not warn the faithful purposelessly lest they receive the grace of God in vain; nor purposelessly does Christ exhort to prayer and watchfulness. But if we hold the difference between the indolent security of the flesh and the tranquil condition of mind born of faith, the problem is soon solved. Believers ought to be sure of their salvation. So that they can lie down and fall asleep? throw themselves down in dull laziness? Rather that, enjoying quiet security with God, they may at the same time watch with prayer. Paul exhorts them to work out their own salvation with fear and trembling (Phil 2.12). So that they may anxiously fear about the issue? Not at all; but that hidden under the wings of God they may continually commit themselves to Him, depending wholly on Him alone, so that relying on His support they may not doubt that in the end they will be victorious. For Paul adds the reason why they are not to be anxious: For it is God that works for His good pleasure both to will in them and also to do (ibid., v. 13). That they should not remain in suspense, he had already removed every doubt from them: He who began a good work in you, will complete it until the day of Christ (Phil 1.6). The Spirit of God, then, never exhorts us to care and application in prayer, as if our salvation fluctuated in a state of uncertainty, for it rests in the hand of God; never imposes on us a fear that cuts away the confidence founded on the gratuitous love of God. By such urgent exhortations the Spirit corrects the indolence of our flesh. For his own purpose, Pighius falsely distorts the words of the apostle in the eleventh chapter to the Romans (v. 20ff.): Because of unbelief, some of the native branches of the olive are broken off; and you by faith are grafted in. Be not lifted up in mind, but fear; for if God did not spare the natural branches, take heed lest it happen that He spare not you. Behold therefore, the goodness and severity of God—to those who fell severity, but to you goodness if indeed you remain in that goodness. After speaking of the twofold election of his own people and showing that the defection of many resulted in the formerly legitimate and proper heirs of life through the covenant established with their fathers being now disowned by God and extruded from His kingdom, Paul turns to the Gentiles, lest they should exult over the Jews for having succeeded to their place. But it is to be observed that, as the universal rejection by his people did not impair God's fixed determination to save a remnant, so the universal election of the Gentiles does not so embrace every individual as to make all sharers of life. Paul here records God's twofold election for the Jews. For in a sense the whole family of Abraham had been elected. But as many were not ordained to life in the hidden judgment of God, the greater number perished, though election still remained with the remnant. Now that the covenant of life is transferred to the Gentiles, that common adoption of the family of Abraham applies to us. But this does not prevent a few from being destined to enjoy it by the hidden good pleasure of God. Paul therefore, when contrasting the Gentiles with the Jews, calls them sterile wild-olives, engrafted into the sacred root when the natural branches have been cut away. He is not dealing with single individuals, nor simply with the hidden election of God. He is showing how great is the reversal of things when children are rejected and strangers are substituted in their place. Hence Paul's whole exhortation is addressed not so much to the faithful who had truly and heartily embraced the grace of God as to the body of the Gentiles which was composed of varying members. Yet there is nothing absurd in God restraining fleshly pride in His children, since they are all burdened with this vice. But what Pighius infers is absurd, that the sureness of divine election depends on the perseverance of men. Even in the general defection of all, the divine election must none the less stand.

VIII.9. *The perversity of the reprobate*

As to the impious who revile the judgment of God in a perverted form, saying that it is vain for the reprobate to apply themselves to righteousness and sanctity because in any case they must perish, the calumny is born of gross ignorance, and I have already brushed it aside with a brief answer.[1] There can be no desire of doing good in men that is not the result of election. But the reprobate, vessels to dishonour as they are, never cease to provoke the vengeance of God on themselves and with evident signs show themselves devoted to destruction.

[1] French has: such as I give in my *Institutes*.

To Pighius[1] this is the height of all absurdities, and he finds nothing so monstrous in all the discussion. But by this one argument he abundantly proves that he is carried away by such a rabid lust for contradicting the truth, that his abuses boil over without occasion. Scripture teaches that none but the elect are led by the Spirit of God. What rectitude can there be in man apart from the leading of the Holy Spirit? The works of the flesh, says Paul, are manifest (Gal 5.19); and elsewhere he pronounces all the thoughts of the flesh to be hostile to God (Rom 8.7). Where then is the absurdity of saying that those not regenerate by the Spirit of God are slaves of sin and carried away by the will of their flesh? Whom God elects, He justifies (Rom 8.7). Is it a wonder that the reprobate who are destitute of the righteousness of God know how to do nothing but sin? God has chosen His own to be holy and without blame (Eph 1.4). If sanctity is the fruit of election, who can deny that others remain sunk in profane uncleanness? Christ declares that none hear His voice but those who are His sheep; and again that they are of the devil who will not hear the word of the Father sounding in His mouth (Jn 10.26, 8.44). To show that the reprobate seek to do good works, Pighius must show that their obstinacy is pleasing to God. Against this, Pighius objects that Saul excelled in many virtues, and was indeed pleasing to God. On my side, I admit that virtues which shine in the reprobate are laudable according to their own nature. This Scripture means by saying that Saul and others of a like kind did what was right. But as God looks upon the heart, which is the fount of works, a work, which is generally and in itself good, may be an abomination to God because of the vice latent in it. This rudiment of piety is unknown to Pighius, that there is nothing so pure that the uncleanness of men will not defile. Hence it is no wonder that, judging Saul's works by their external appearance, he should commend his innocence and probity. When he contends that Saul did once please God, I make a distinction. For God so honoured him with royal office that in Scripture the house of Israel never censured him, as Ezekiel testifies (Ezek 13.9). But because Judas is elected to apostolic office, will Pighius conclude that he is therefore numbered among the children of God? Pighius deliberately distorts what I have said,

[1] To Pighius . . . occasion—French has: Pighius and the like seethe with rage against this reply; but I can without difficulty show that they fight against God.

as if I spoke of single and individual actions of life and not rather of the whole course of life. In a word, all Scripture totters, if we do not allow that whatever righteousness and goodness can be found in men proceeds from the Spirit of sanctification given to the sons of God alone.

VIII.10. The supposed ill-effects of Predestination

I shall not spend much more time in pursuing the rest of his petty objections. The next is a commonplace: Teaching is vain and exhortations empty and useless, if the strength and power to obey depend on the election of God. Another is similar: It must be that men give themselves up to indolence, when they are taught to rest in the eternal counsel of God. Pighius is wont to attack the answers given by me with such abuse that I must save them from being handled by him again.[1] But there may be some people, more than usually peevish and not yet satisfied, with whom Augustine has greater weight. I will therefore repeat and confirm what I have said in his words. His words are found in the work entitled *De Dono Perseverantiae*.[2] They will say that the doctrine of predestination is hostile to preaching and renders it useless. As if this objection could tell against the apostle and his preaching! Did not this doctor to the Gentiles commend predestination times without number and never cease to preach the word of God? He said: It is God that works in you both to will and to do (Phil 2.13); did he therefore not himself exhort us both to will and to do what pleases God? Because he said (Phil 1.6): He that began a good work in you will complete it, did he stop persuading men to begin and to complete the work to the end? Nor is His opinion false and His definition vain when Christ says: No one comes to Me, that is, no one believes in Me, unless it is given him by My Father (Jn 6.44). Nor again because the definition is true is the precept false. Why must we say that the doctrine of predestination is useless for preaching,[3] exhortation and correction when Scripture commends the one as much as it makes use of the other? And shortly after: Those hear these things and do them to whom it is given; but those to whom it is not given do them not, whether or not they hear them. Preaching of persevering and efficient

---

[1] French has: The replies which I have given above ought to be enough for Christians; and in fact those who contest them are unable to find fault with them.

[2] Cap. 14.   [3] The chief authority has falsely: predestination.

faith is not to be held up by predestination, so that they may hear what they ought and that they to whom it is given may be obedient. For how shall they hear without a preacher? Nor again is the preaching of predestination to be held up by the preaching of efficient faith that perseveres to the end, so that those who live faithfully and obediently may not glory in that obedience as though it were their own, but rather in God. And again: as he that receives the gift, rightly exhorts and preaches, so he that receives the gift obediently hears the exhortation and preaching. So our Lord says: Who has ears to hear, let him hear. As for the question from whom they have the gift that have it, our Lord Himself replies: I shall give you a heart to know me and ears to hear me. Ears for hearing, then, are the very gift of all obedience, and all endowed with it come to Christ.

Therefore we both exhort and preach. Those who have ears to hear, hear us obediently; in those who do not, what is written is fulfilled: That hearing they may not hear (Is 6.9); for they hear with the bodily sense but not with the assent of the heart. But why do some have and others not? that is, why is it given by the Father to some that they should come to the Son and not given to others?—Who has known the mind of the Lord? Must we deny what is evident because we cannot comprehend what is hidden?

Augustine continues:[1] How preposterous then is the caution of those who for fear of some absurdity would suppress or obscure a doctrine so necessarily known! Suppose that some on hearing it give themselves up to torpor and stagnation and readily exchange labour for licence according to their desires; is what is said about the foreknowledge of God to be therefore thought untrue? Would not these have been good if God had foreknown they would be good, however much they now revel in wickedness? And if He had foreknown them to be evil, will they not be evil, whatever the goodness with which they now appear? Are the truths about the foreknowledge of God to be denied or hushed up because of such cases? when all the time it is known that, if they are not declared, other errors would arise? A reason for being silent about the truth, says Augustine,[2] is one thing; the necessity for speaking it another. To seek out all the reasons for not speaking the truth would be a long business. But this is one, namely, that we should not make

---

[1] Ibid., cap. 15.   [2] Cap. 16.

worse those who do not understand while wishing to make wiser those who do. By our saying such things, they may not be made wiser, but neither are they rendered worse. But where the fact is that he who does not understand is made worse by our speaking, and he who can understand by our silence, what is to be done? Is it not better to speak the truth, so that he who is able to understand may understand, than to be silent,[1] so that not only do both not understand, but also that he is made worse who is more intelligent—he from whom, if he heard and understood, others might learn? Then we should be unwilling to say what Scripture allows to be said. Our fear would be lest by our speaking he should be offended who is unable in any case to understand, not lest by our silence he should fall into error who is able to understand the truth. This opinion he elsewhere touches upon more briefly but confirms more clearly.[2] Wherefore if the apostles and the teachers of the Church who followed them both piously declared the eternal election of God and at the same time held the faithful within the discipline of the pious life, why should the men of our day, convinced by the vehemence of truth,[3] think it right to say that, though what is said about predestination is true, it should not be popularly preached? The doctrine ought indeed to be preached forthrightly, so that he that has ears may hear. But who has these ears who has not received them from Him who promised to give them? Let him who does not receive the truth reject it; but let him who understands take and drink, and drink and live. For as piety is to be preached, that God be rightly worshipped, so also predestination, that he who has ears may hear of the grace of God and glory not in himself but in God.

Yet there was a singular devotion in this saintly man to edification, and he tempered the system of teaching the truth, so as prudently to avoid offence when permissible. For he advises that the things said are to be consistently said.[4] If anyone should force people thus: If you do not believe, it is because you are destined by God to destruction, he would not only foster his own idleness but also indulge his malice. If anyone

[1] French has: than to weaken and keep it concealed.

[2] Ibid., cap. 20.

[3] French has: why it is that those are convinced by the truth should think it right to say, etc.

[4] Ibid., cap. 22.

again should extend his opinions into future time, saying that those who hear never will believe because they are reprobate, this would be imprecation rather than doctrine. Such men Augustine orders to be expelled from the Church deservedly as foolish teachers and sinister and ominous prophets. Elsewhere[1] he contends that it is when one is sympathetic and helpful that he profits others in correction, when he induces those he wishes to benefit without rebuke. But why some profit and others do not, far be it from us to say that it is the judgment of the clay not of the potter. Again later:[2] When men by rebuke come or return to the way of His righteousness, who works salvation in their hearts but He who gives the increase, let who will plant and water? When He wills to save, the free will of no man can resist Him. Hence there can be no doubt that human wills are unable to resist the will of God who did what He willed in heaven and earth and has done even things future, or prevent Him doing what He wills, seeing that He does with the wills of men themselves what He wishes. Again, when He wishes to bring men, does He bind them with physical chains? He works inwardly, takes hold of their hearts inwardly, moves their hearts inwardly, draws them by the wills which He has wrought in them. But what Augustine adds in continuation[3] must not be omitted. Since we do not know who belongs to the number of the predestined and who does not, it befits us so to feel as to wish that all be saved. So it will come about that, whoever we come across, we shall study to make him a sharer of peace. But our peace shall rest upon the sons of peace. Hence, so far as we are concerned, salutary and even severe rebuke will be administered like medicine, lest they should perish or cause others to perish. But it will be for God to make it effective in those whom He foreknew and predestined.[4] If these things are true and have the testimony of the first of the holy fathers, let them not be spewed out in hatred upon Calvin[5] by the ignorant and ill-affected. Would that those insipid and moderate ones, who too much please their own tearful sobriety, would just consider how much Augustine, to whom they allow knowledge of sacred matters, is also their superior in modesty, so that they should not pass off their morose timidity as modesty.

---

[1] *De Corrept. et Gratia ad Valent.*, cap. 5.
[2] Cap. 14.   [3] Cap. 15.   [4] Cap. 16.
[5] French has: in hatred of myself.

VIII.11. Reprobation and the goodness of God

Now to deal further with Pighius. My readers are reminded of three summary particulars. First, however many absurdities he gathers to injure my doctrine, he pits himself not so much against me as against God. Next, in twisting the passages of Scripture which clearly support me, he trifles ignorantly and, as appears plainly, is unable to sustain his case without corrupting and distorting Scripture. Lastly, he rushes into such impudence, that he does not hesitate to summon Augustine to his aid. If God created any for destruction,[1] He is not worthy to be loved. Those who are deprived of eternal life before they were born are more worthy of pity than of punishment. If the views he tries to overturn were mine, he would be fighting against a mortal man; but since it is God whom he openly insults with these infamies, I am not ashamed to repeat a hundred times with Paul: O man, who art thou that contendest with thy maker? This miserable man feels now, and those like him will one day feel, that the reproaches their profane and sacrilegious mouths hurl at God collapse by their own impetus before reaching heaven, nor do they come to rest except by recoiling on their own heads. To give one example of this detestable madness in perverting Scripture: the ninth chapter to the Romans, which he partly confuses and partly dismembers. To begin with,[2] to save himself trouble in cutting this Gordian knot, he severs it with one word. Israel is elect, but not all Israelites, because they do not represent their father who received his name by seeing. Hence he infers that election is only ratified in those who open their eyes. But in interpreting the name Israel, this good master of perspicacity is ludicrously blind. He is making a sharp point out of a blunt log. Meantime he does not consider that Israel was divinely made by peculiar grace, since he was elected in his mother's womb. Nor are others capable of seeing God, unless He illumine their minds. And only those are deemed worthy of the light of the Spirit whom He adopted as sons for Himself when they were

[1] French has: As to the first point, he says that God is not worthy of love, etc.

[2] French has: Firstly, when St Paul speaks of election, this good glossator says: Israel was elect, but all descendants of the race are not Israelites. Now he blindly deceives himself if he hopes to escape thus. For he does not consider that Jacob was truly made Israel by a special grace, in that he had been already elected in his mother's womb. Upon this, he comes up again, saying that the mercy of God is lacking to none that is, etc.

still blind. After this, Pighius, like someone escaping, jumps all the fences in his path. The mercy of God is lacking to no one; for God wills all men to be saved, and He stands and knocks at the door of our hearts, desiring entrance. Therefore, those were elect before the foundation of the world whom He foresaw would receive Him. But He hardens no one except in for-bearance, just as too easy-going fathers are said to spoil their children by indulgence. As if by such trivialities it was possible to escape what Paul distinctly affirms to the contrary, as if it meant nothing to his readers[1] that of two twins still in the womb one should be elected and the other rejected, without respect to merits but solely by the good pleasure of God who calls; that it is not of him that wills or him that runs but of the merci-ful God who hardens whom He will and shows mercy to whom He will; that God shows His power in the vessels of wrath, so that He might make known the riches of His grace in the vessels of mercy; that whatever of Israel is saved is saved according to gratuitous election; and that so election obtained it (Rom 11.7); not to speak of all we have expounded above in due order! If Pighius were a thousand times more acute, he would not by his trifling objections prevent even the deaf from hearing the resounding voice of Paul. With[2] all his amassing of words, he is left with this mountain: God did not create reprobates whom He foreknew to be such, but knew some to be reprobates whom He had created. This is as if he smeared the eyes and the hands of the potter with clay, lest His form should be apparent to us. Similarly when he sets himself to expound the first chapter to the Ephesians. He sports and flourishes his bombast as if to strike Paul dumb with his inane clamour. God chose us in Christ, because He foresaw in us a place for His grace which was otherwise free to all. He elects from the whole, because He foresaw that what was set forth in common for all would become peculiarly ours, that sanctified by it we might be co-operators. He chose according to the purpose of His will, which is and was that He should choose those of whose future He foreknew what was written. He chose to the praise of His grace which sanctifies us, as praise belongs to the perceptor and the teaching and its benefit to the disciple. As

---

[1] French has: as if by such bandages he was able to bind the eyes of all the world, so that one sees nothing more in the text of St Paul. But this doctrine is far too clear to divert readers so easily.

[2] With all . . . apparent to us—lacking in French.

if[1] that were not the purpose of God which elsewhere (II Tim 1.9) Paul opposes to all human works! As if in the term good pleasure there were not in this passage a more express commendation of grace! As if God were not said to have purposed His good pleasure in Himself alone, because finding no cause in us He made Himself the cause of our being saved! As if it was in vain that Paul repeats five times that our salvation is wholly the effect of that decree and purpose and good pleasure! As if he declared without any purpose that we were blessed in Christ because we were elect! As if he did not derive sanctification and any good works there may be from election, like water from a fountain! As if he did not refer to the same grace the fact that we are God's handiwork, made for good works which He prepared! As if He did not distinguish us from the rest, in order that we might know we excel all others by the gratuitous favour of God alone! Look then, how[2] fitly foreknowledge of works agrees with the Pauline text! How much better it would have been to have retained the role of an admirer of the apostle, which for a moment he was forced to assume but soon laid aside when he turned to haughty speculations! But these matters I have handled more fully above and now only briefly touch.

VIII.12. Man's will and God's grace

Pighius afterwards scourges Augustine severely for showing in this subject more impetuosity than calm reason, striking here and there, and proposing things evidently alien to the goodness of God. Then he shamelessly uses his support. This I shall show with three words. He praises the diligence of the holy man for having so carefully winnowed this question in his book written to Simplicianus, Bishop of Mediola. Whether he ever looked into the work I do not know. For he makes it out to be one book instead of two. It is remarkable that this good and dexterous interpreter should from all his works have preferred to single out this, which, as Augustine himself records, was written at the beginning of his episcopate. For although the author wrote it against Pelagius, he does not disguise the fact that he discussed the same matter much more fully and

---

[1] French has: He babbles with I know not what audacity, as if, etc.

[2] Look then . . . touch—French has: See then the fine solutions Pighius brings me as the testimonies of Scripture—the rest omitted.

solidly later.[1] These are his words: The predestination of the
saints is there set forth by me. But later necessity compelled
me to defend the doctrine with greater diligence and labour,
when I was disputing against the Pelagians. For we have said
that particular heresies brought into the Church their own
questions; and against these Scripture has to be defended more
diligently than if no such necessity had arisen. But let us see
what kind of adherence it is that Pighius gives to Augustine.
He is with us, he says, in affirming that the cause of reprobation is the rejection of calling. In fact, Augustine thinks quite
otherwise. For in the *Retractations*[2] he says that he worked for the
free will of man, until the grace of God conquered. But I omit
what he says there and in two other passages already quoted,
though indeed my exposition of his thought is more reliable
than a thousand like passages of Pighius. How does Pighius
have such impudence as to refer to him opinions which in all
his work he not only strongly rejects but frankly condemns?
In brief, the words Pighius adduces as supporting himself do
indeed appear in Augustine, but they are refuted on the very
same page.[3] He says: Scripture declares it is not of him that
wills nor of him that runs, but of God that shows mercy. If the
reason is that the will of man is not alone sufficient for us to
live righteously and uprightly unless it be assisted by the mercy
of God, then we might as well say it is not of God that shows
mercy but of man that wills; for then the mercy of God is not
alone sufficient unless the consent of our will is added. But it is
manifest that our willing is vain unless God show mercy; but
I do not know how it can be said that the mercy of God is vain
unless we will. For if God have mercy, then we will, because it
belongs to that mercy to make us will, according to the Scripture: It is God who works both to will and to do. For if we ask
whether a good will is the gift of God, surely no one will dare
deny it. A little later Augustine says: Hence, the truth is that it
is not of him that wills or of him that runs, but of God that
shows mercy, because even if He call many yet He has mercy
only on those whom He so calls as to make the call effectual in
them so that they follow it. But it is false for anyone to say:

[1] *De Praedest. Sanct.*, cap. 4; *De Dono Persev.*, cap. 20.

[2] *Retract.*, lib. 2, cap. 1.

[3] About half way through lib. 1 [the reference seems to be to *De Diversis Quaes-
tionibus* ad Simplicianum, mentioned by Calvin above, lib. 1, quaest. 2, §1.]

It is not of God that shows mercy, but of man that wills, because God has mercy on none ineffectually. When God has mercy on anyone, He so applies the call to him that he does not reject the caller. What Pighius said by way of preface is therefore quite true: Augustine has indeed winnowed the question now discussed. But he sins grievously in snatching at the chaff blown about in the air and neglecting the wheat left visible by the fan.

IX. Georgius

IX.1. Georgius: Election has different senses

Now[1] some space must be given to Georgius of Sicily also. Everything about this man is so insipid that I feel ashamed to spend time on his refutation. Nor should I think it worth while coming to grips with this shadow, did not the foolish consternation shown by many force me. Nor do I think there will be wanting those who, seeing me win so easily a victory over such puerile trivialities, will deride such a useless investigation. Indeed, did he not, as I hear with great grief, do mischief, I should think he ought to be met with contempt rather than explicitly refuted with words. But since his books fly about Italy, driving many people to distraction on every side, I would rather myself play the madman with this crazy fellow for a little than by silence allow the Church to be attacked in such furious assaults.[2] Formerly when the prophet Ezekiel saw certain old prophetesses deluding the people, he was not ashamed to declare war on women (Ezek 13.17). Therefore, if we would serve Christ, let us not be grieved to engage and disperse any that try to throw their chaff into the granary of the Lord.

When we say that men are predestined by the eternal counsel of God either to salvation or to destruction, Georgius thinks that we are deluded in the matter for three reasons. The first he assigns is that we have not observed that the word election is used in Scripture in different senses. God elects

[1] French has: Now it is right that the monk Georgius should come into the picture, and that we should see the fine arguments which he adds to those of Pighius, for ruining the election of God with regard to the faithful. I should not deign to amuse myself with such trash, were it not that I see the devil taking advantage of it to trouble greatly the poor ignorant and weak among us, and that by this means he greatly harms the Church, etc.

[2] French adds: We see that St Paul was not ashamed to address himself to a smith who pitted himself against the Gospel.

certain people to temporal office where there is no mention of
eternal life and no thought of it. But how will this stupid
trifler show that we are so inexperienced in Scripture as not to
hold that Saul, who was reprobate, was none the less elected
king (I Sam 9.16)? that Judas, one of the twelve whom Christ
declares He chose, is called a devil (Jn 6.70)? Why does he not
point out passages of Scripture wrongly and impiously adduced
by us which will show up our error? In fact he makes up
dreams for himself, the children of his own brain, and battles
with them as though they belonged to another. Meantime he is
remarkably forgetful of his own precept in about the tenth
section, when he opposes Paul's testimony to us: Lest, when I
have preached to others, I myself should be a castaway (I Cor
9.27). For he infers from this passage that either Paul is lying
in expressing the fear that the immutable election of God
might fail; or[1] that he was uncertain about his own election.
This miserable man does not see that reprobate or disapproved
is opposed to approved, that is to those who had given proof of
their piety. How does it not occur to him that there are different
meanings for reprobate? For the reprobate silver of Jeremiah
(6.30), and the reprobate earth of the Epistle to the Hebrews
(6.7), do not mean silver and earth devoted to destruction but
debased and worthless silver and unfruitful earth. But that in
Paul's words the reference is to men, as also in another epistle
(II Cor 13.6), is evident from the context. Yet so unmistakable
is the difference between eternal election, in which God adopts
us to life, and election to temporal office, that Scripture sometimes joins them together because of their affinity. When Paul
glories in being separated from his mother's womb (Gal 1.15),
he is speaking of the apostolic office; but rising to a higher
level he equally praises the grace of God by which he was
called to the hope of salvation. Christ too, though He calls one
of the twelve whom He chose a devil, elsewhere joins the grace
of adoption with the apostolic office, saying (Jn 15.16): You
have not chosen Me, but I have chosen you, and ordained you,
that you may go and bear fruit, and that your fruit may remain.
By this principle He declares that His own were given Him by
the Father, that He might allow none to perish, except him who
was the son of perdition (Jn 17.12). Thus we everywhere read
that people are elected to a certain kind of life or a certain

[1] Beza and Amst. have the bad reading: and.

temporal office; but this does not alter the fact that God elected for salvation those whom He willed to be saved.

IX.2. Georgius: Election is on the basis of faith

The second cause of our error which he gives is that we do not hold all the faithful of the New Testament whom He calls to be elected to salvation, though Paul teaches this in the first chapter to the Ephesians. But we have more than sufficiently demonstrated that the faith by which the children of God enter into possession of their salvation is there derived from election as its origin. Faith is certainly to be specially reckoned among those spiritual riches given to us in Christ. But what does Paul teach to be the origin of all the blessings we have but that hidden source of gratuitous adoption? Again: Wherein He abounded to us in all knowledge and prudence—how? According to His good pleasure which He purposed in Himself. If the fruit of divine election is faith, it is evident that not all are illumined to faith. Hence, it is established beyond doubt that those on whom God decreed in Himself to bestow faith are chosen by Him. Thus Augustine is right when he writes: Men are elected to be God's children in order that they might believe, not because He foresaw that they would believe.[1] I pass over other passages that might be cited, because they too will have to be considered. But there is one passage where the elect of God seem to be regarded as an infinite number, that is where Christ predicts so many fallacies of Antichrist that, if it were possible, even the elect would be deceived (Mt 24.24). Georgius explains the elect in this passage to mean those who persevere in faith and righteousness. This is indeed correct, provided that their constancy be made to depend on their election. But to exclude any kind of special election in God, Georgius makes each man himself the author of his own election.[2]

IX.3. Georgius: Scriptural blindness is punishment

The third cause of our error, according to Georgius, is that, while Scripture speaks of blindness and hardening, we do not take notice that these are the punishments of even greater sins. But we do not deny what is expressed in countless passages of Scripture: God punishes, with blindness and in other ways,

---

[1] *De Praedest. Sanct.*, cap. 17, and elsewhere.
[2] This last sentence is wanting in some versions.

contempt of grace, pride, stubbornness and other crimes. For the notable punishments of which mention is everywhere made ought to be referred to the general principle that those who have not duly feared God and reverenced Him as is fit are given over to a reprobate mind and handed over to shameful lusts (Rom 1.26). This will be dealt with at greater length later. But, though the Lord strike the impious with madness and consternation and so repays them the reward they have deserved, this does not alter the fact that there remains in the reprobate a blindness and obstinate hardness of heart. When it is said that Pharaoh is hardened, he was already worthy to be handed over by God to Satan. But Moses also testifies that he was first raised up by God for this very purpose (Ex 10.20). Nor does Paul adduce any other cause than that he was one of the reprobate (Rom 9.17). Paul shows the same thing when the Jews, deprived of the light of understanding,[1] fell into horrible darkness and thus suffered the just punishments of their wicked contempt of divine grace. Nor does he conceal the fact that this blindness was inflicted on all the reprobate. For he teaches that the remnant were saved according to gratuitous election, and all the rest were blinded (Rom 11.5). If all the rest, whose salvation is not governed by the election of God, are blinded, it is clear that the same people who provoked the wrath of God by their rebellion and procured fresh blindness for themselves were already from the beginning devoted to blindness. The words of Paul are plain (Rom 9.22): the vessels of wrath are first prepared for destruction, those that is, who, destitute of the Spirit of adoption, precipitate themselves into destruction by their own fault. With Augustine,[2] then, I do not hesitate to confess that something always precedes in the hidden judgments of God, but it is hidden. For how God condemns the impious and also justifies the impious is shut away from human understanding in inaccessible secret. Hence there remains nothing better than in awe to exclaim with Paul: How unsearchable are His judgments, and His ways past finding out (Rom 11.33).

IX.4. Georgius' denial of particular election

Georgius then proceeds:[3] No syllable in all Scripture can be found to justify the conclusion that those who were

---

[1] French has: light of life.   [2] *Contra Faust.*, lib. 21, capp. 2 and 3.
[3] French has: When the monk has offered so fine a preamble, he says.

reprobated by the eternal judgment of God were blinded. All we say about predestination is so much philosophical sophistry. For nothing of the future is hidden from God; and whatever He foresaw necessarily comes about. I say nothing to this, except that our works refute so gross a falsehood.[1] The fact is that the favour of the reverend abbot gave this man licence to give vent within his little fraternity to whatever he might imagine, as though it were oracle; and he let himself expect the same thing outside the monastery.[2] But we do not draw the distinction between elect and reprobate, against which Georgius vainly fights, from the bare foreknowledge of God, as he falsely represents. Must I now with further words say that it is proved by the manifest and consistent witness of Scripture? He represents us as fighting from the bare concept of divine foreknowledge. But readers will find more than twenty clear passages of Scripture cited above by me.[3] He objects that particular election is a fiction of our own, for God chose no certain individuals. But Christ declares on the contrary that He knows whom He has chosen (Jn 13.18).

See, then, how strong are the weapons with which he shakes that eternal counsel of God by which some are elected to salvation and others destined for destruction. Paul indeed makes the righteousness of God common to all who believe. He admits no distinction, for all have sinned and come short of the glory of God (Rom 3.22). With all my heart I allow that the righteousness of God is extended to all through faith. But from where does faith come, except by the gratuitous illumination of the Spirit? And whom does Paul consider as believing in Christ, but those whom the heavenly Father has drawn (Jn 6.44)? Christ certainly counts none among His own, unless he be given by the Father; and He declares those to be given who before were the Father's (ibid. 17.6). Georgius here obtrudes his delirium about natural faith, which it is not my present purpose to refute. I will only say that the righteousness of God is to all and upon all who believe in Christ. But with Paul as witness I say that, where some excel others, the difference is from God alone, lest anyone should glory (I Cor 4.7). Further, that we may know the things given us by God, our

---

[1] This sentence is wanting in the French.
[2] French has: to fill the world with lies from his printed books.
[3] But readers . . . by me—wanting in the French.

eternal inheritance is sealed in our hearts by the earnest and pledge of the Spirit (II Cor 1.22). Further, that we may believe is given us by God (Phil 1.29). Further, the eyes of our understanding are enlightened to know what is the hope of our calling (Eph 1.18). Further, the fruit of the Spirit is faith (Gal 5.22). Paul says there is no difference (Rom 3.23), but he means between Jews and Greeks, because God invites both equally to salvation. But these two races, says Georgius, comprehend the whole of mankind. Let it be so. He cannot thus prove that righteousness is promised particularly to every individual man. Suppose we grant this last point, we must return to the fact that no one can become a partaker of the good offered him but by faith. It remains for the monk to make faith common to all. This I have sufficiently proved to be contrary to the mind of Paul. But then, he will persist,[1] only the elect will have come short of the glory of God. How does he gather this? Because, he says, the grace of Christ is poured out on all who have sinned.[2] But I hold the grace of God to be so universal, that I make the distinction to consist in this, that all are not called according to God's purpose.[3]

IX.5. Christ the propitiation for the whole world

Georgius thinks he argues very acutely when he says: Christ is the propitiation for the sins of the whole world; and hence those who wish to exclude the reprobate from participation in Christ must place them outside the world. For this, the common solution does not avail, that Christ suffered sufficiently for all, but efficaciously only for the elect. By this great absurdity, this monk has sought applause in his own fraternity, but it has no weight with me.[4] Wherever the faithful are dispersed throughout the world, John extends to them the expiation wrought by Christ's death. But this does not alter the fact that the reprobate are mixed up with the elect in the world. It is incontestable that Christ came for the expiation of the sins of the whole world. But the solution lies close at hand, that who-

---

[1] French has: he objects that there follows the great absurdity.

[2] French adds: that necessarily all are chosen or rather that only the chosen have sinned.

[3] French adds: St Paul speaks of this, implying a certain movement of the Holy Spirit.

[4] This sentence is omitted in the French.

soever believes in Him should not perish but should have eternal life (Jn 3.15). For the present question is not how great the power of Christ is or what efficacy it has in itself, but to whom He gives Himself to be enjoyed. If possession lies in faith and faith emanates from the Spirit of adoption, it follows that only he is reckoned in the number of God's children who will be a partaker of Christ. The evangelist John sets forth the office of Christ as nothing else than by His death to gather the children of God into one (Jn 11.52). Hence, we conclude that, though reconciliation is offered to all through Him, yet the benefit is peculiar to the elect, that they may be gathered into the society of life. However, while I say it is offered to all, I do not mean that this embassy, by which on Paul's testimony (II Cor 5.18) God reconciles the world to Himself, reaches to all, but that it is not sealed indiscriminately on the hearts of all to whom it comes so as to be effectual. As for[1] his talk about no respect of persons, let him learn first what the term person means, and then we shall have no more trouble in the matter.

But Paul teaches that God wills all to be saved (I Tim 2.4). Hence, it follows that God is not master of His promises, or that all men without exception must be saved. If he should reply that God, so far as He is concerned, wills all to be saved, in that salvation is offered to the freewill of each individual, then I ask why God did not will the Gospel to be preached to all indiscriminately from the beginning of the world. Why did He allow so many peoples for so many centuries to wander in the darkness of death? For the context goes on to say that God willed all to come to the knowledge of the truth. But to the candid reader of sound judgment, the sense is quite clear, as I have expounded it above. Paul has enjoined solemn and general prayers to be made in the Church for kings and princes, lest anyone should have pretext to deplore the kings and magistrates for being at the time violent enemies of the faith. He deals with this situation, and affirms that the grace of Christ is open to this kind of person also.

It is not to be wondered that the more this worthless fellow distorts Scripture the more passages he gathers; for he possesses

---

[1] As for, etc.—this, though in the original, is lacking in the French which runs: This mischief-maker assembles many passages to which there is no need to reply in particular. Above all, he so twists and turns as to confuse even himself without convincing others. I have already answered one part of what he says. I will only touch briefly on what could perplex simple people. He cites a passage of Isaiah, etc.

no religion or shame to restrain his impudence. But the more diffuse he is, the more brief I shall make my replies. He cites Isaiah (56.3): Let not the son of the stranger say, I am rejected; and he takes for granted that this cannot be applied to the reprobate. He thinks it absurd that the elect should be called the sons of a stranger. I reply that it is not unusual to find that those elected before the foundation of the world are thought of as strangers, until by faith they are gathered among the sons of God. The words of Peter are borrowed from the prophet: Who were formerly not a people, but are now the people of God (Hos 2.23; I Pet 2.10). Who are addressed? Surely those whom, at the beginning of the Epistle, he had testified were the beloved according to the foreknowledge of God the Father (I Pet 1.2). Even clearer is the Epistle to the Ephesians. After discussing their election, he adds that they had been exiles from the kingdom of God, strangers to the promises, without God or hope of life (Eph 2.12). Is it any wonder that Isaiah, building the temple of God with profane stones, declares that there will be a new consecration? For since the calling of the Gentiles was hidden in the heart of God, what else appeared in them but damnable impurity? In this sense, therefore, they were exiles and strangers. But, as many as were at last incorporated into the body of Christ were God's sheep, as Christ Himself testifies (Jn 10.16), though formerly wandering sheep and outside the fold. Meantime, though they did not know it, the shepherd knew them, according to that eternal predestination by which He chose His own before the foundation of the world, as Augustine rightly declares.[1]

Georgius continues: If the word of the prophet be true, the son shall not bear the iniquity of the father (Ezek 18.20), then no part of mankind is left in original sin.—I really wish to have nothing to do with this monster. My purpose is to assist the inexperienced, lest they be enticed by such trivialities. Nothing is more certain than that whoever is not engrafted into the body of Christ is left in the general destruction. This fine monk, generous to the stranger as he is, brings all together, and makes members of the household those to whom God closes and bars the gate. But it is madness not to say that those who are naturally dead in Adam are unable to be restored to life unless a divine remedy be applied. Paul clearly states the difference

[1] *Tract. in Ioann.*, 45.

between the seed of the believing and the seed of the unbeliev-
ing man: the former is holy and the latter unclean (I Cor 7.14).
On this principle, before the wall was broken down and the
Gentiles incorporated with the Jews in the Church, he declares
that the branches of Abraham are holy from their holy root
(I Cor 7.14).

What need is there of long discussion? Did not the prophet
Ezekiel, whose word this monk misuses, frequently assign the
peoples, uncircumcised and profane, to destruction (Ezek 28.10;
31.18, 32 et passim)? Neither would circumcision be then the
covenant of life on any other grounds.[1] How then can it be
true that the son will not bear the penalty of the father's guilt?
And on the other hand I ask how any man will boast himself
innocent who is born an unclean raven from an unclean egg.
For original sin is so contracted from Adam that it becomes
a property of each man. No one can therefore rightly complain, as if he innocently bore the guilt of another's sin.[2] But
if it is not permissible for God to punish in the sons the sins
of the fathers, what does this mean?: Punishing to the third and
fourth generation (Ex 20.5; Deut 5.9); and again: Visiting
the sins of the father upon the sons (Ex 34.7, etc.). So the first
part of this vengeance is that they be destitute of the Spirit
of God and remain in their natural pravity.

John says (Rev 3.5, 22.18): Whoever has sinned, I shall
delete him from the book of life. If, says Georgius, you apply
this to the reprobate, they never were written in the book of
life; if to the elect, the counsel of God is unstable.[3] So babbles
this monk, as if God did not always accommodate Himself to
our understanding. What base ingratitude to reproach God
for being so indulgent to us that He prattles for our sake! By
this reasoning, he will render us a corporal God because
Scripture ascribes eyes, feet and hands to Him! But the meaning
is simple: those are deleted from the book of life who, considered for a time to be children of God, afterwards depart to
their own place, as Peter truly says about Judas (Acts 1.16).
But John testifies that these never were of us (I Jn 2.19), for if
they had been, they would not have gone out from us. What
John expresses briefly is set forth in more detail by Ezekiel

---

[1] French has: as sure sign of the alliance of God.

[2] French adds: since all are tainted with evil and merit condemnation.

[3] French adds: He then concludes that there is no certain election.

(13.9): They will not be in the secret of My people, nor written in the catalogue of Israel. The same solution applies to Moses and Paul, desiring to be deleted from the book of life (Ex 32.32; Rom 9.3): carried away with the vehemence of their grief, they prefer to perish, if possible, rather than that the Church of God, numerous as it then was, should perish. When Christ bids His disciples rejoice because their names are written in heaven (Lk 10.20), He signifies a perpetual blessing of which they will never be deprived. In a word, Christ clearly and briefly reconciles both meanings, when He says: Every tree which My Father has not planted will be rooted up (Mt 15.13). For even the reprobate take root in appearance, and yet they are not planted by the hand of God.

The comparison of Paul (Rom 5.12ff.), says Georgius, is to be noted. As by one man sin came into the world to condemnation, so also by one man is the gift of righteousness to life. If in one man, he says, many died, much more must the grace of God abound that many through Christ may reign unto life. If Paul were there maintaining that the grace of Christ extended to all, I should in silence own myself vanquished. But since his purpose is to show how much more powerful in the faithful is the grace of Christ than the curse contracted in Adam, what is there here to shake the election of those whom Christ restores to life, leaving the others to perish? But this monk[1] calls attention to the words; for Paul comprehends all the race of men, when he says that the sin of one man came upon all, and hence no one may be excluded from participation in life. If it were permitted to reason in this way, I should contend that God must then create new worlds, that there things might be managed better than here. Christ declares that the curse was not equal to the grace, which much exceeds it. If the number of men affected be everywhere reduced to this standard, Christ could not save more than Adam lost. Therefore the faith of Paul is imperilled, unless a new world should immediately arise. But I shall oppose the monk with the very shield he offers me. He adduces another passage from Paul: As in Adam all die, so in Christ shall all be made alive (I Cor 15.22). If the second part of the text is extended to all the sons

---

[1] But this monk . . . in life—French has: It is true that St Paul comprehends the whole human race, from which this monk infers that it is not permissible to exclude anyone and that all enjoy the grace brought by Jesus Christ.

of Adam, Paul interposes his hand. For he explicitly testifies
that he speaks of members of Christ only. Christ the firstfruits; then also will rise those who are Christ's. He certainly
speaks here of the resurrection, which is followed by a blessed
immortality such as we confess in the faith.[1]

IX.6. The Gospel rightly preached to all

But that I should not vainly fatigue my readers by repetition,
I propose to take up a few matters out of many. I have shown
above in what sense God wills not the death of a sinner, when
willing that all should be converted and live. For when He
exhorts men to repentance and offers pardon to the converted,
this is common to all. But He deems His own children worthy
of the privilege of having their stony hearts made hearts of
flesh. Nor do I concede to the monk[2] that these words are
spoken vainly into the air, so long as the Lord leaves the
wicked convicted in their sins and inexcusable, but so works
in His elect that the hidden doctrine becomes effectual in their
hearts by virtue of the Spirit as it sounds in their ears. Nor is
there any reason why that common falsehood should distress
anyone, which suggests that God mocks at men by exhorting
them to walk when their feet are tied. For He does them no
injury in demanding nothing but what they owe. Unless of
course the bankrupt with nothing with which to pay may
boast, in derision of his creditor, that all is discharged.[3] But I
will not pursue further a strife which cannot be resolved,
except by the conscience of each man. God commands the
ears of His people to tremble at the voice of His prophet
(Is 6.9). That their hearts may be touched? Rather that they
be hardened. That those who hear may repent? Rather that
the already lost may perish twice over. If you reply that something greater was at stake,[4] I ask for nothing more in the
present instance. It is not absurd that by this command of God
doctrine should be spread abroad which He knows will lack
effect. Not less frivolous is the objection that the word of Christ
is inconsistent with election, when He speaks of the sheep

---

[1] The last words omitted in the French, as is also the first sentence of the following paragraph.

[2] French adds: Now how is it that God does not vivify the heart of each one,
if I do not agree with this monk that the general promises are frustrated, etc.

[3] French has: a careless liver, spending all his goods.

[4] French adds: and God punishes the sins committed.

brought back after it was lost. But it is much more appropriate for me to throw back the missile which he tried to hurl at us. The reason for its being a sheep apparently lost for a time is precisely that with respect to election it remained in the custody of God all the time.

Of the same kind of stuff is the dilemma he poses. If there be any special election, the exhortation of the prophet will not square with it: Let the wicked forsake his way (Is 55.7). For if it be addressed to the elect, how can they be wicked in whom all things work together for good? if to the reprobate, how can they be called to repentance? I answer that the appeal of the prophet is addressed to both; to the former, that those among them who have thrown off the yoke and trespassed may return to a sound mind; to the others, that, stupefied in their evil, they may be pricked by such a stimulus. For we do not imagine that the elect always hold to the right course under the continual direction of the Spirit; we say that they often fall, err, suffer shipwreck, and are alienated from the way of salvation. But since the protection of God by which they are defended is stronger than all, they cannot fall into fatal ruin. Men are bidden to take care lest they perish. But it is certain that the elect are beyond peril, while the reprobate will not be warned. I reply that there is no absurdity. The elect, who are engaged in perpetual conflict, must be furnished with necessary arms, and the vigilance of all is stimulated; while the reprobate prove themselves at length to be incurable. For medicine is administered in diseases until hope is given up.

Georgius objects: Abraham is called father of the faithful, not of the elect; and salvation is promised not to the elect but to those who believe. Whom then does he say those are who are gathered with their father Abraham into the kingdom of God? For Christ certainly teaches that this belongs to the elect alone. Christ declares that an end will be imposed to the awful disasters for the sake of the elect (Mt 24.22; Mk 13.20). Shall we deny that those are children of Abraham who are along with him made members of the household of the Church? How is it, pray, that such honour was bestowed upon Abraham that he should be reckoned the father of the faithful, except because he was elect of God? How is it that those are accounted degenerate children[1] who in this regard do not correspond to

[1] French has: illegitimate children.

him? The audacity of this worthless person is indeed execrable; for he strives with all his might to efface and blot out the mark by which God chiefly distinguishes His children. I certainly allow that eternal life is promised to those who believe, provided that he in his turn does not deny that it is similarly promised to the elect (for so Isaiah (65.9): And my elect shall possess it). Let him only admit that only those believe whom God illumines by His Spirit; only confess that election is the mother of faith. Paul declares that he is prepared to suffer all things for the elect's sake (II Tim 2.10). Christ proclaims that the Father is the avenger of the elect (Lk 18.7). Paul exhorts the Colossians that as the elect of God they put on gentleness, patience, and all the other virtues (Col 3.12). Paul, too, exempts all the elect of God from guilt (Rom 8.30). Are the faithful to be robbed of these goods? As if between things mutually and indeed inseparably joined together there should be a worse than hostile disagreement. No; that the election of God may stand, those formerly blind are illuminated into faith; and by faith they receive the righteousness of Christ; and by faith they are kept to the end.

IX.7. *How the reprobate cause their own destruction*

Georgius proceeds: When Scripture pronounces destruction for the lost, it does not at all refer or trace back the cause to the eternal counsel of God, but testifies that it resides in themselves. But we do not represent the reprobate as being so deprived of the Spirit of God that they may find the fault of their crimes in God. Whatever sins men commit, let them impute them to themselves. If anyone should evade this, I say that he is too strongly bound by the chains of conscience to free himself from just condemnation. Let Adam excuse himself as he may, saying that he was deceived by the enticements of the wife God gave him; within himself will be found the fatal poison of infidelity, within himself the worst counsellor of all which is ambition, within himself the diabolical torch of pride. Hence they will be quite inexcusable who try to elicit from the profound recesses of God the cause of their evils, which in fact operates from their own corrupt heart. They deserve to be given over to a reprobate mind (Rom 1.28), who did not as they ought glorify God in the aspect apprehensible in the heaven and the earth. Those who wilfully and with deliberate malice reject the grace of Christ and do not hesitate to reject the shining light of the Gospel, will suffer the heavier punishment. Let each acknowledge his own sins, condemn himself, and, confessing from the heart all his guilt, supplicate in humility his judge. If anyone object, the answer is immediate: The destruction is thine own, O Israel. For, as we have elsewhere said, if, according to the ancient poet, Medea complains foolishly in lamenting that the timber was ever cut in the Pelian grove,[1] while all the time it was the internal fire of her lust that ruined her father and his kingdom along with herself, much less will they be heard who assemble far remote causes from the clouds to cover the knowledge of their guilt, which all the time lies deep in their own hearts and cannot remain hidden. Therefore Scripture rightly assigns the cause of all evils to sin. The dispute between us is not whether men perish by the hidden judgment of God beyond their deserts. This we declare to be false and detest as a foul sacrilege. The dispute is whether the ungodly who voluntarily provoke the wrath of God upon themselves were before divinely reprobated by a cause which was just though unknown. Now Paul severely condemns the sins of men, powerfully stirs up their conscience, and skilfully vindicates the righteousness of God from the sacrilegious falsehoods of men. So also he declares that those who precipitate themselves into ruin were vessels prepared for destruction (Rom 9.22). Christ, too, charges the reprobate with deserved guilt. But at the same time He says they were trees not planted by the hand of the Father (Mt 15.13). In a word, we learn that the Father gives those who are His to the Son, that He might sanctify them (Jn 17.6). On the other side, Paul, after teaching that the election of God was attained, submits that the rest are blinded (Rom 11.7). Hence the error of Georgius is that, fixing his eyes on sins that are manifest, he never considers their hidden source in the corrupt nature of man.

Georgius thinks we are involved in absurdity, because we make man free to sin, while the reprobate sin of necessity. But the freedom of which we speak, because it is too familiar to him, is not really known by him. Paul calls some free who are free from reverence for righteousness and without fear of God revel

---

[1] French has: the complaint which the daughter of the ancient king made, that the timber had been cut to build the ship on which had come a young man with whom she had fallen in love, etc.

in intemperance (Rom 6.20). Does it follow that these are not servants of sin? He accuses us of limiting the power of God, because if God knows and ordains all the future he is not then able to alter it. Truly a prodigious marvel, that God should not show Himself like a mortal man, variable and flexible and changing His counsels every hour![1] For what does this monk so violently attack but that God should necessarily be consistent with Himself? But his error is that, by separating the fixed decrees of God from His power, he divides Him against Himself. To speak in Stoic terms, there is the well-known sentiment of Seneca: God is necessity to Himself.[2] With greater reverence and soberness, we would say: God always wills the same thing, and this is the praise of His constancy. Whatever He decrees He effects, and this agrees with His omnipotence. His will is joined with His power, constituting a symmetry worthy of that providence which governs all things.

I have nothing to say about the different and contradictory testimonies from Scripture which Georgius puts together. We may spare his ignorance but must curb his impudence lest it should distress simple people.[3] From one passage of Paul, he shows that God sends the spirit of error upon rebels who decline to obey the truth, so that they believe falsehood (II Thess 2.11). He then adduces another different passage: the doctrine of the Gospel is hidden to those that are lost, whose minds the god of this age has blinded (II Cor 4.3). I admit, indeed, that these are called unbelieving. But if unbelief is the sole cause of their blindness,[4] what is the meaning of what follows, that God who commanded the light to shine out of darkness has shined in the hearts of the faithful? We know that darkness is everywhere; but God brings light out of darkness.[5] As for the accusation of cruelty because we obstruct the way of salvation for ourselves and many others, while Christ Himself most kindly invites the Canaanite woman and the lost sheep and even the strange dogs, my reply is that we faithfully set

[1] French adds: but remains firm and constant when once determined—the following sentence omitted.

[2] French adds: By this he signifies that there is no compulsion from outside, but that He constrains Himself to will immutably to do what He does.

[3] This sentence is wanting in the French.

[4] French has: the voluntary malice by which they resisted the Gospel after hearing it.

[5] French adds: This appears in those who believe; but the unbelieving have a blindness deeper and more profound than that which proceeds from their rebellion.

forth all the doctrine of faith and penitence committed to us that all may profit by Christ. When our Lord was Himself asked by the wife of Zebedee to place her sons, the one on the right and the other on the left, He curbs her foolish and untimely desire, saying that this did not agree with His present vocation; but He makes it clear that a place is decreed for each by the heavenly Father who in His time will make it evident (Mt 20.21; Mk 10.35). In the same way, the superstition[1] which Scripture makes evident ought not to be covered up by our silence. Until the day of revelation come, we are to do what our Lord commands and exhort all without exception to faith and penitence. For the doctrine is common to all, and is deposited with us for this end,[2] until the reprobate by their deplorable obstinacy block the way.

IX.8. Election precedes faith and perseverance

Forced to admit that predestination is attested by so many passages of Scripture, Georgius throws up a new objection, more foolish and rotten than can be imagined. The faithful of the New Testament are said to be elected by God in that it is to them that He makes known the riches of the mystery hidden from all ages. In this sense, he collects all the texts that declare the excellency of the grace shown in Christ. Then he concludes that whatever the first chapter to the Ephesians contains is only to be understood as meaning that God deems the faithful of the New Testament worthy of this peculiar treasure. As to the time to which this grace refers, he teaches that it is made common to all men from the advent of Christ to the end of the world. But the words of Paul reveal a quite different conception. They amount to this, that only those are illumined to faith who were predestined to life according to the eternal good pleasure of God. It cannot be denied that there was then a special calling of particular persons. Nor was the Gospel preached to all. Suppose it granted that it sounded by the external voice in the ears of all; Paul here refers to a higher calling by which the Spirit of God penetrates hearts. But the distinction between internal and effectual calling and external calling Georgius declares to be all a dream. The experience of faith, however, amply testifies how little frivolous is a distinction

---

[1] French has: predestination.
[2] French adds: with this intention, that it be offered to one and all.

of this kind. Paul here treats election in no other sense and for
no other end than elsewhere, when he gives thanks to God for
having from the beginning elected the Thessalonians to salvation
(II Thes 2.13), thus distinguishing a small part from an ungodly multitude. Georgius replies that the lawless despisers of
grace are opposed to the elect. But this is not to the point.
All I at present contend for is that some are specially chosen
in preference to others; while Georgius on the other hand
babbles that we are predestined only in the sense of being born
at a certain time.[1] What about Judas? He was given to hear
Christ and to enjoy His intimate fellowship; yet Christ
denied that he was elect. I speak not of all, He says, for I know
whom I have elected (Jn 13.18). But if this fanatic be credited,
the condition of Herod is better than that of David; the impious scribes will have precedence in honour of election to the
holy prophets, for, he will say,[2] the latter are not of the number
of the faithful. Everywhere he insists that the grace of election
belongs in general to a certain age; and, wishing a guarantor
for his credibility, he declares that Paul never spoke otherwise
of predestination. What?[3] Does he include all the men of his
age when he affirms that those are justified whom God has
predestined (Rom 8.29)? Does he not rather separate from
the rank and file those that are called according to the purpose?
Further, when he elsewhere says that God chose the foolish
things to confound the wisdom of the world (I Cor 1.27), does
he apply to his whole age so manifest a discrimination?

But feeling himself caught, he tries another refuge.[4] Those
are not called elect whom God preferred to others, but rather
such as persevere in the common election and grace. By this
he means that those who distinguish themselves from the
multitude of men by constancy of faith are at length deemed
elect. He cites a passage from Paul: I charge you before God
and the elect angels (I Tim 5.21). As if what he demands could
be allowed him, that, because they did not fall away with the
apostate, they would therefore attain the grace of election!

[1] French adds: at which Jesus Christ appeared; from which he concludes that
there was no difference between good and bad.

[2] For, he will say . . . faithful—for this, the French reads: since election is only
for the later time.

[3] French has: But I do not know who will be so foolish as to credit him.

[4] French has: The monk does not mind if he contradicts himself or makes use of
another subterfuge to develop his thought.

But the contrary proposition, that they stood fast because they were elect, is ever so much more probable. Let there be no dispute about a word. When Christ predicts that the deceptions of Satan will be so great as, if it were possible, to lead the elect into error (Mt 24.24), He implies that it is quite impossible for Satan by main force to carry off the elect. By what virtue shall we say that they are secure? Georgius supposes that they stand by their own strength. But Christ judges very differently: No one will pluck from My hand the sheep committed to My charge; for the Father who gave them to Me is greater than all, and no one can pluck them from the Father's hand (Jn 10.29). So Paul is far from enjoining the faithful to trust in their own constancy; he reminds them that God is faithful who called them, and who also will do it (I Thes 5.24). Georgius makes each one the author and arbiter of his own salvation; but Christ testifies that those whom He chose out of the world are His own (Jn 15.19). With this view Paul agrees: All things work together for good according to the purpose (Rom 8.28); and of infants not yet born: That the purpose of God to election might stand, not of works but of Him that calls; as it is written: Jacob I have loved (Rom 9.11). Nothing is left for this worthless fellow, except to babble that Jacob while in his mother's womb obtained the honour of election by his industry and stood possessed of it to the end by his constancy.

Just as much reason is there for[1] the suggestion that the rejection, about which Paul speaks, refers not to individual persons but to the whole body of the Jewish people; since that people in rejecting Christ deprived themselves of the inheritance of eternal life. Now I allow that this is the originating cause of the dispute. But no sane person will conclude that the whole question is restricted within these limits. For Paul teaches that the race of Abraham consisted of both elect and reprobate. Further, he declares in general that there come from the human race vessels of wrath and vessels of mercy for the manifestation of the glory of God. Paul indeed defines the proximate cause of reprobation as unbelief of the Gospel; nor do I deny that this is a cause expressly stated by Paul, but only after having first distinguished this factor from the hidden judgments of God. For he deals with two distinct things: that

[1] French has: There is the same impudence in.

God was never so bound to one people as to prevent His free election operating in the choice of rejection of individuals; and also that the Jews by their ingratitude abdicated from the family of God, though they were the legitimate heirs of eternal life. But lest the alteration in God's purpose should disturb anyone, as though this later rejection shook the hidden counsel of God, Paul immediately observes that the gifts and calling of God are without repentance, and that hence the remnant according to gratuitous election is saved (Rom 11.29). By these words is meant that election, founded upon the hidden counsel of God, remains fixed and stable. There is impudence even more base in the suggestion of this worthless fellow that Esau was not reprobated before he sold his birthright. Certainly I admit the word of the apostle (Heb 12.17), that when he had deprived himself of his inheritance, he was rejected. Did then his father's rejection of him which he then suffered do away with the higher judgment of God?[1] Certainly no more than did the faith and obedience of Jacob overturn the gratuitous adoption of God.

I repeat what I said at the beginning. No one can disprove the doctrine I have expounded except he who pretends to be wiser than the Spirit of God. Now,[2] however, the sour resistance of men reaches such a height that they will not quietly and willingly receive what is evidently taken from Scripture, without arrogating to themselves the prerogative of God, namely, the right to impose a law of speech and silence. Yet some wish to conceal this under the guise of modesty, professing that they would not dare to deny what is testified by all the servants of God. For my part, I soberly and reverently confess that I know no other law of modesty than that which I have learned in the school of the heavenly Master. But I am not unaware that prudence should be shown in tempering everything to the building up of faith. But as I have studied in good faith to do just this, even if the niceties of some are not yet satisfied, I fancy I have done my duty. He that has ears, let him hear.

[1] French has: But the apostle means what he says, that his rejection was already apparent. This is not to say that God had not already judged him. On the contrary, we see that the faith and obedience of Jacob did not merit his being adopted by God.

[2] So all the Latin editions. But the French reverses: Never—which wholly agrees with the thought of the author and should be restored in the original. In one edition of the text, there is a pen correction: Never.

X. PROVIDENCE

X.1. Definition of providence

By His providence,[1] God rules not only the whole fabric of the world and its several parts, but also the hearts and even the actions of men. A mass of literature confronts anyone who will write on this subject. But since I have already so dealt with the subject as to give considerable satisfaction to sound and fair readers, I shall summarise it now with as much brevity as is possible. It cannot be hoped that what I say will match in splendour the greatness and excellence of the subject. I shall refer in a few words to what was expounded at greater length in my *Institutes*; and, if authority is needed, I shall attach scriptural proof. Thus I shall dispose of the sinister and malignant observations of Pighius and others like him, which evilly distort what is well said, lest pious minds should be hindered or disturbed.

We mean by providence not an idle observation by God in heaven of what goes on in earth, but His rule of the world which He made; for He is not the creator of a moment, but the perpetual governor. Thus the providence we ascribe to God belongs not only to His eyes but to His hands.[2] So He is said to rule the world in His providence, not only because He watches the order of nature imposed by Himself, but because He has and exercises a particular care of each one of His creatures. For it is indeed true, that, as the creation of the world was beautifully ordained by the admirable wisdom of God, so it is unable to persist in being unless it be sustained by His virtue. That the sun should daily rise for us, that in its swift course it has degrees so fitly tempered,[3] that the separate orbits of the stars are wonderfully undisturbed, that the seasons continually recur; that the earth yields its annual produce for the nourishment of men, that the elements and particles do not cease to discharge their office, that finally the fertility of nature never fails as though it were fatigued—this

[1] In the French alone, there is this inscription: Concerning Providence in General. In the Latin original, only the titles of the columns, as they are called, or pages change.

[2] French adds: that is to say, He does not only contemplate what He has made, but cares for His work as seems good to Him.

[3] French has: none the less within certain limits better than any clock.

is to be ascribed solely to His directing hand who once made all things. Psalm 104 is nothing but a eulogy of this universal providence. So too Paul declares, when he says that in Him we live and move and have our being (Acts 17.28). Since this is the essential property of the one God, so faith must consider the secret vitality it communicates, by which it comes about that creatures exist, though they will also soon perish.

X.2. Particular application of providence

But knowledge of universal providence is by itself vague and confused, unless at the same time we hold that God embraces individual creatures in His care; as Christ also teaches when He says that not even a little sparrow, sold for half a farthing,[1] falls to the ground without the will of the Father (Mt 10.29). In this special providence which watches over the individual works of God particularly, it is convenient to determine certain distinct grades. For since man is the most noble work of God, for whose good everything which heaven and earth contain was made, Scripture chiefly commends to us the providence of God in governing the human race. Paul in expounding the passage: Thou shalt not muzzle the mouth of the treading ox (I Cor 9.9), says that oxen are not a concern to God; which means that He does not preoccupy Himself with their care, though it is within His competence, but rather concerns Himself with man. But because God deals here with men equipped with reason, the reason of His providence manifests itself more certainly and clearly. For His judgments show themselves wonderful, whether for punishing crimes, or instructing the faithful in patience and the subduing of the flesh, or purging the vices of the world, or rousing many from indolence, or opposing the pride of the ungodly, or deriding the stratagems of the wise, or demolishing the machinations of the wicked. On the other side there is reflected His incomparable goodness in assisting the wretched, protecting and defending the safety of the innocent, and bringing help to the despairing. Of this providence which concerns men, there is a beautiful description in Psalm 107. For there the prophet shows that what in common estimation are thought whims of fortune, are in fact so far from being imposed by blind chance, that they clearly mirror the goodness or the wrath or the

[1] French has: for a farthing.

justice of God. So he concludes: If they will prudently consider
what changes of fortune take place in the world, it will be a
matter of joy to the godly; such examples of the works of God
are potent enough to shut up the mouth of the wicked (Ps
107.42).[1]

X.3. Providence specially directed to the Church

But here again there are degrees of direction. For though
God shows Himself father and judge of the whole human race,
yet, since the Church is the sanctuary in which He resides, He
there displays His presence with clearer evidence; and there
performs the office of father of His family, and honours it, as
I may say, in its proper aspect. Scripture refers to testimonies
of this kind when it affirms that God keeps even closer watch
over the faithful (Ps 33.18). The Lord keeps watch over the
souls of His saints (Ps 97.10).[2] God cares for you (I Pet 3.7).
The hairs of your head are all numbered (Mt 10.30). For the
Church is God's own workshop, in which He exercises His
providence—the chief theatre of the same providence. For the
same reason it is said that the angels, who are as it were His
hands, have been appointed watchmen for His faithful (Ps
34.8), lest they should be in any way separated from the body
of Christ whose members they also are. Therefore, to put the
matter within the comprehension of the simple, there is first
to be asserted before the eyes of all the general government of
the world, by which all things are cherished and nourished,
so that their natural state may remain intact.[3] Then there are
to be considered the guards God sets for the government and
care of particular parts—of such a kind, indeed, that nothing
happens but by His will and assent. Then there must come to
mind His particular care of the human race, by which it
comes about that the life and death of men, the condition of
public kingdoms and peoples no less than of private individuals,
and everything commonly ascribed to fortune, all depend upon
a single heavenly control.[4] Lastly, there is the truly paternal

---

[1] French adds: Then he adds that it is great wisdom to come to this conclusion,
in order that we may the more carefully apply our study (ibid., v. 43).

[2] French inserts: He does not allow the righteous to be ever overcome (cf.
perhaps Ps 37).

[3] French has: though created for a moment only.

[4] French has: this is the true reference for all that men attribute to fortune; in
brief, it is there that the whole condition of men should be referred.

protection with which He guards His Church, to which the
most present help of God is attached.[1]

X.4. Exposition of providence requires discretion

No words can worthily and sufficiently express how great
and how diverse is the usefulness of this doctrine. No one can
profitably weigh up what Scripture testifies to us about the
providence of God in governing the world, or what is known
by means of faith, unless he reminds himself that he has here
to do with his maker and with the creator of all things, and
first submits himself in fear and reverence of such majesty[2]
as befits humility. For if anyone is accustomed to have honour
from his equals, so that he candidly and modestly judges in
matters concerning them that are obscure or insufficiently
known, sedulously enquires their significance, and prefers to
suspend judgment rather than by too much precipitation to do
injury, would it not, I ask, be a more than monstrous enormity to show less discretion and to measure the works of God by
our standards,[3] investigate His hidden counsels, and trifle in a
profane way with mysteries so great and so profoundly ador-
able?[4] But if such petulance has rioted in all ages, it displays
itself much more insolently today than ever before. And many
Epicureans, as we may call them, because they are unable to
drag God down from heaven, show their godless rage in trying,
by deliberation and example, to expel at least His worship and
all religion from the conscience of themselves and all others,
by emitting detestable and unworthy blasphemies. But for the
most part, the origin of the evil is clearly this, that superficial
and impetuous spirits indulge primarily their own frivolous
curiosity, so as to set themselves no limit and to apply themselves to quite empty speculations. Then unbridled audacity
arises, and stimulates other tongues to emulate their lack of
moderation with their petulance. Others attempt the same
thing, having different faults but doing no less injury. For,

[1] French adds: which is joined and united with His own by means of His Son.

[2] French adds: which ought to make us tremble in His sight. Anyone proceeding
with such modesty will learn what profit and reassurance there is in apprehending
by faith that God governs the world. On the other hand, audacity and temerity
will only render us blind and deaf.

[3] French has: at the bar of our judgment.

[4] French adds: and in babbling without consideration as if they were only
worthless trash.

implicated in absurd fancies, they destroy their minds voluntarily either in desperation or in carelessness.[1] It is the device
of the devil to involve pious and sound doctrine in monstrous
fictions,[2] and so not only to snatch from us its enjoyment, but
also to render it partly hateful and partly disastrous. But,
whatever he attempts, a warning will show us that it is all
perverse; for, as they run into such dangers, they find no other
summary principle, than to corrupt or obscure what is simply
set forth in Scripture.

X.5. The end of providence a proper confidence

The remedy is much more fitting: to learn how and for
what end the providence of God is to be understood. The first
end is to divest us[3] of rash confidence, so as to hold us in the
fear of God and then to arouse us to invoke Him. The second is
to teach us to rest in God with quiet and tranquil minds[4] and
to despise with confidence and courage the perils that surround
us and the hundred deaths that threaten us. Let me expound
both items. When men imagine that anything is fortuitous, or
ascribe anything to their own industry, wisdom, wealth, or
human assistance, proceed audaciously to attempt all things,
strive, travel all over, move some mountain, and constantly
think up something novel, as though free to wander in empty
space,[5] then there is no invocation of God and no fear. But
where men acknowledge their purpose and the issue of all
things to be governed by the providence of God, admit fear-
fully with Jeremiah (10.23): I know, O Lord, that the way of
a man is not in himself, nor is it for man to direct his footsteps;
thinking like Solomon (Prov 20.24): The steps of a man are
from the Lord, and what man will dispose his way?, there they
subject themselves wholly to the Lord and depend upon Him.
Then there follow prayers, that God may begin and complete
in us whatever works we confidently undertake. Similarly the
man who invents an empire of chance or the devil,[6] relaxes the

---

[1] French has: they are consciously careless or are driven to despair.

[2] French adds: confusing it among foolish comments and absurdities.

[3] French adds: and knowing that we can do nothing, but that all is from the
hand of God, let us be humbled to fear, etc.

[4] French adds: in the confidence that He will conduct our affairs well.

[5] French has: they behave like an unbridled horse in a spacious and beautiful
countryside.

[6] Beza and Amst. have the bad reading: or as for the devil.

reins for the ungodly and other brute beasts, as if they were able to do anything outside the assent and ordinance of God— he will continually fret with miserable anxiety, will turn his life round and round as though it were suspended by a thread, and will hardly dare to move a foot, lest he should despair of life.[1] But the faithful, since they set before themselves the directing hand of God, will not hesitate to cast all their cares upon Him. And as they know that the devil and all the ungodly, however much uproar they may make, are not only tied fast by the chains of God but even compelled to render Him obedience, they will proceed quietly on their way.

X.6. Providence refers to past as well as future

Two other distinctions add some light. The first is that the providence of God is to be referred to past as well as future time; the other, that, sometimes with and sometimes without and sometimes contrary to all means, the highest power is to be ascribed to Him who ordains and creates all things. To consider the reference to past time: if anything follows according to one's wish or desire, let mortal man not sacrifice to his own net, as Habbakuk says (1.16), nor exalt his prudence or virtue or good fortune; let him not make the offering to men or creatures which is properly God's own. But let him be persuaded that God is the prime author of his blessing, however it come about. But in adversity, let him rest in this consolation: As God pleased, so it has come about; by revolting against God, I profit nothing and only involve myself in the guilt of impious contumacy. Then let the memory of his past life come before him, so that, from the punishments inflicted upon him, he may learn his sins. As for future time, the providence of God is to be thought of in this way by pious minds. There is always an intention in His promises and threats. If there should be any discrepancy, there will remain no building up in the fear of God and no progress in faith. But the man who observes the omnipotence of God in the mirror of His word will not only rise above the innumerable perils of the world on the wings of faith, but also be less subdued and humiliated by daily aggravations. When I said that the providence of God is to be considered along with the means employed, I meant, that if anyone give help to those who

[1] French adds: in a word, he will be as though numbed.

labour in the last extremity, the deliverance is not human, but divine by the hand of man. The sun rises daily, but it is God that gives light to the earthly globe. The earth produces fruit, but it is God that supplies bread and by bread imparts vigour to us in our need. In a word, when inferior causes, like veils, withdraw God from our sight, as they usually do, we must penetrate higher by the eye of faith, so as to discern God's hand working in these instruments. Christ teaches by an example how to look away from the means and give place to the providence of God, when He repelled the assault of Satan with the shield: Man does not live by bread alone, but by every word that proceeds from the mouth of God (Mt 4.4). For, as He knew the power of God needed no external support, He concludes that it is supplied without bread as well as being mercifully supplied by bread. Hence, we are to guard against being so attached to inferior means, as to think that the hand of God alone by itself cannot supply us abundantly with all help. Apart from mere means, the providence of God attains its deserved praise from us, when we are persuaded that it is superior to all obstacles[1] and we conquer all assembled terrors by faith alone. For this is a real wrestling school in which God tests our faith, for every day obstacles arise to impede His counsel up and down through all creation. What then is to be done? If only faith will ascend to the level of divine power, it will without great trouble overcome all agents that seem to oppose it.

X.7. God the cause of all happenings, yet not the author of evil

Whoever continues in such godly fear will not worry himself with devious speculations, nor because he knows that all things are divinely created will he think this a pretext for ignorance, nor yield to desperation, nor fly off to frivolous nothings and things unworthy of God's majesty. But now there arises the question of the origin of these battles. We are not to think that the providence of God, rightly understood, generates them out of itself. The cause is rather that, in thinking about the works of God, human reason is blind and prone to disputation.[2] But it is no wonder if the counsels of God, which the angels

---

[1] French adds: and, though all creation revolts against God, He will in the end make His will prevail.

[2] French has: . . . as though it squinted, being half blind . . . if it so bother, skirmishing here and there and rushing about in this direction and in that.

look into from the height of heaven (I Pet 1.12); are little congruous with the flesh. But it is an insufferable wickedness to think that we, who can hardly crawl on the earth, should take nothing as true except what submits itself to investigation by our eyes. But care is needed, if the doctrine is to be fruitful in fortifying the simple and inexperienced and in refuting the falsehoods of the ungodly.[1] First, it must be observed that the will of God is the cause of all things that happen in the world; and yet God is not the author of evil. I will not repeat here with Augustine what yet I willingly accept from him as true: There is nothing positive in sin and evil:[2] for this subtlety does not satisfy many. For myself, I take another principle: Whatever things are done wrongly and unjustly by man, these very things are the right and just works of God. This may seem paradoxical at first sight to some; but at least they should not be so offended that they will not suffer me to search the word of God for a little to find out what should be thought here. But lest we should look with pride and stubbornness, as if it were proper for God to fit Himself to our standards, we must first listen to Scripture, where the whole definition of the works of God is to be found.[3]

That God directs by His counsel the things that seem most fortuitous, is clearly attested by Scripture when it says: The lot is thrown into the lap, but the judgment of things is from the Lord (Prov 16.33).[4] Similarly, if a branch cut from a tree, or an axe slipping unintentionally from a man's hand, strike a passerby on the head, Moses testifies that God did it on purpose, because He willed the man to be killed (Ex 21.13). Other Scriptural evidence I omit for the time being, because the thing is so expressly pointed out. But because the necessity of Stoicism seems to be established by what is said, the dogma is hateful to many who would not dare to call it false. The calumny is an old one, and Augustine complains that he was frequently charged with it falsely.[5] But it ought now to be

---

[1] French adds: so far as they can discuss the truth.

[2] French has: evil and sin are nothing in themselves but only a disorder or corruption of what ought to be.

[3] French adds: As for sin, I protest that I wish to ascribe nothing to God out of my own brain; but we must leave with Him what are His proper attributes.

[4] French adds: If there were any cases of chance, these would be: but we see that they are governed by God from above.

[5] *Ad Bonif.*, lib. 2, cap. 5.

regarded as obsolete. It is certainly unworthy of honest and wise men, if only they be properly instructed. The nature of the Stoics' supposition is known. They weave their fate out of a Gordian complex of causes. In this they involve God Himself, making golden chains, as in the fable, with which to bind Him, so that He becomes subject to inferior causes. The astrologers of today imitate the Stoics, for they hold that an absolute necessity for all things originates from the position of the stars. Let the Stoics have their fate; for us, the free will of God disposes all things. Yet it seems absurd to remove contingency from the world.[1] I omit to mention the distinctions employed in the schools. What I hold is, in my judgment, simple, and needs no force to accommodate it usefully to life. What necessarily happens is what God decrees, and is therefore not exactly or of itself necessary by nature. I find a familiar example in the bones of Christ. Scripture testifies that Christ assumed a body quite like our own. That its bones were frangible no sane man doubts. But another and distinguishable question seems to arise here, whether any bone of His could be broken. For all things must necessarily remain intact and unimpaired because they are so determined by the fixed decree of God. And though I shrink from the received forms of speech, and the distinction between absolute and consequential necessity, I use them, but only lest any subtlety should prevent even the most simple of my readers from understanding what I say. Hence, considered naturally, the bones of Christ were frangible; but considered in the decree of God, which in His own time was manifested, they were no more liable to fracture than angels to the troubles of humanity. But though it is proper for us to regard the order of nature as divinely determined, I do not at all reject contingency in regard to human understanding.

X.8. God's use of inferior causes

Further what I said before is to be remembered, that since God manifests His power through means and inferior causes, it is not to be separated from them. It would be foolish to think that, because God has decreed what is future, all care and endeavour on our part is rendered superfluous. If there was anything that we must do, He prescribed it, and willed us

---

[1] French has: as for what is called contingency, it means that things can happen either in one way or another.

to be the instruments of His power; and it is right for us not to separate what He has joined together. In the beginning, He commanded that the earth produce all kinds of herbs and fruit without the aid of human art or cultivation; but He now invites the hand of man and works by means of it. If anyone boast that he expects to have bread by mere idle desire, because it is the blessing of God that makes the earth fruitful, does he not simply spurn the providence of God in preaching such an understanding of it? For this is to separate and distinguish what belong together by divine connection. Hence as to future time, because the issue of all things is hidden from us, each ought so to apply himself to his office, as though nothing were determined about any part. Or, to speak more properly, he ought so to hope for the success that issues from the command of God in all things, as to reconcile in himself the contingency of unknown things and the certain providence of God. And God promises His blessing to the labour of our hands. By this word, the pious man comprehends that he is constituted an instrument of divine providence. Supported by this same promise, he girds himself for the work with alacrity,[1] because he is persuaded that his pains are not airily thrown to chance, and that as he puts his trust in the word of God he will be directed to the best of ends by His secret counsel. Then, since the providence of God as rightly expounded does not bind our hands,[2] so it does not discourage invocation but rather confirms it. Whatever happens, it is right to temper our judgments with the same soberness as in past time. There is no more apt exhortation to patience than to hear that nothing occurs fortuitously and that what seems good to God will be done. Meantime it does not follow that the blame for the adversity of things is not carried by our laziness or temerity or thoughtlessness or any other vice. If it be not right to think that the things that happen, happen without any reason, as often seems to be the case, no pious minds will cease to ascribe praise to the wisdom and justice of God.

X.9. Man's counsels overruled by God

But where it is a matter of men's counsels, wills, endeavours, and exertions, there is greater difficulty in seeing how the

---

[1] French has: to put one's hands to the dough, as one says.
[2] French has: to make us idle or lazy.

providence of God rules here too, so that nothing happens but by His assent and that men can deliberately do nothing unless He inspire it. The clear evidence of His providence daily shows how He relaxes the reins to the foolish counsels of men, and yet, concealing from them the means He uses, He frustrates them in the last resort. But Scripture praises His strong hand and dominion in another direction, when He is shown inflaming the ungodly, striking them with giddiness, and driving them into madness or stupefaction; or again weakening their hearts and filling them with terror, so that they collapse at the sound of a falling leaf. Pighius too little considers this, and restricts God within too narrow limits; whereas, like a prudent man[1] or a general expert in military affairs, He foresees the plans of His enemies and counters them with timely measures. Both things are expressly stated: He seizes the wise in their craftiness, takes away the spirit of princes, and makes their prudence vanish (Job 5.13; Ps 76.13). Gross, too, is the lack of perception which denies that the man who is killed by the deliberation of men dies by the will of God, merely because where the will of man interposes the action of God is not present.[2] What then of the innumerable passages of Scripture which testify that the swords of the wicked are overruled by the hand of God? Were the sons of Eli killed without human intention (I Sam 4.11)? But there is a eulogy given, because God willed to kill them. For that God overrules the hands of men, now binding them and now directing them here or there for the execution of His purposes, no one of even mediocre acquaintance with the Scriptures will call in question. But it is accepted almost universally by common sense that, though men may labour, the issue is in the hand of God. But because of the dense darkness of the human mind by which all knowledge is rendered thin and perishable, Scripture builds for us a higher watch-tower from which to observe God overruling all the works of men so as to direct them to the end appointed by Him.

It comes to this, that though men wanton like untamed animals bound by no ties, yet they are ruled by a secret rein so that they cannot move a finger without performing God's rather than their own work. As for the faithful who render spontaneous obedience to Him, they are like angels, reckoned

[1] French adds: who can destroy the grass under the feet of His enemies.
[2] Lib. 8, cap. 3. Beza amends: is judged.

as His hands. It is of this chiefly that I would remind those
who never think that they have a concern in the counsel of God
or a relation to His will. Indeed the ungodly pride themselves
on being competent to effect their wishes.[1] But the facts show
in the end that by them, unconsciously and unwillingly, what
was divinely ordained is implemented. Further, God sometimes uses the ungodly like scourges for the punishment of
men's sins; and sometimes He forces them, as though He took
and twisted them round, to be ministers of His benefits. To
assemble the examples of first kind would be an immense task;
but a few may be mentioned. After inciting Assyria to war and
calling it the rod of His anger (Is 10.5), He teaches that it is
equipped with nothing less than the staff of His wrath. Then
He attacks their pride, for not acknowledging that they are the
axe or saw wielded from elsewhere. On these grounds, they are
said to be sanctified by God, to be His conscripted soldiers,
and to render Him assistance. From another point of view it
is their own ambition and cruelty and avarice that impels
them; yet God on His side testifies that with whistle or trumpet-
call it is He that calls them to arms. One passage from Moses
shows clearly enough how the way is prepared for the benefits
of God by the misdeeds of men. The conspiracy of Joseph's
brothers when they sold him was a worse than perfidious and
cruel crime. But, from another point of view, the cause of his
being sold is transferred to God: It is not you but God who sold
me, that I should give you food (Gen 45.5). It follows then that
God operates even through those who act impiously, so that
they find life in death. As far as lay in them, they had killed
their brother; yet from this, life shone forth for them. Similarly
with the prince of crimes and the head of the impious, Satan
himself. God had sent him to deceive Ahab with the design
that there should be a lying spirit in the mouth of all the
prophets (I Ks 22.23). So this spiritual impostor for the wrath
of God is minister for the blinding of the impious who would
not tolerate the truth. On the other hand, Paul, lest he should
be proud in the greatness of revelation given to him,[2] records
that he was given a messenger of Satan to keep boxing him on
the ear (II Cor 12.7). The poison of Satan is the antidote and
remedy for pride. What kind of a doctor, I ask, can Satan be,

[1] French adds: as if they had conquered God and were masters of all.
[2] Lest . . . given him—lacking in all but the chief edition; French includes.

who learned only to kill and to destroy? But God, who commanded the light to shine out of darkness (II Cor 4.6), has marvellously brought salvation out of these depths, as it appears, and turned darkness into light. What Satan does, Scripture affirms to be from another point of view the work of God. By this is meant that God holds Himself bound in obedience to His own providence and turns His face so that He may direct attention to His own ends.

X.10. God moves in the hearts of the ungodly

However, even if Scripture did not present one way of solving this problem, it would not be really difficult to find another. More arduous is the other question: Does God work in the hearts of men, directing their plans and moving their wills this way and that, so that they do nothing but what He has ordained? We do not ask here whether He inspires the pious and holy affections in their hearts, for about this there is no controversy. The question is whether He has in His power also the depraved affections of the ungodly, moving them here and there so that they will what He has decreed they should do. Certainly when Solomon declares (Prov 21.1) that the heart of kings are in the hand of God so that He inclines it as He pleases, he shows that in general the will not less than external works are governed by the determination of God. Moses says that the heart of Pharaoh was hardened by Him (Ex 4.21, 7.3). It is useless to have recourse here to the concept of permission, as if God were said to do what was done only in the sense that He allowed it. For clearly Moses says that the hardening was a work of God. Nor indeed is the savagery of Pharaoh ascribed to God in any other sense than is the grace which He is elsewhere said to give to His people in the eyes of the Egyptians (Ex 3.21). For who does not see that fierce beasts were being tamed and subdued by the power of God, when the Egyptians were suddenly turned towards clemency? We ask, then, how it comes about that Pharaoh should rage so inhumanely, unless it so pleased God, partly to show His tolerance towards His own, and partly to exercise His power. On the same principle it is said that God turned the hearts of enemies in hatred towards His people (Ps 105.25). But this does not prevent it being said elsewhere that Pharaoh himself aggravated the condition of his heart (Ex 8.32). We do not make the minds of men to be impelled by force external to them so that they rage furiously; nor do we transfer to God the cause of hardening, in such a way that they did not voluntarily and by their own wickedness and hardness of heart spur themselves on to obstinacy. What we say is that men act perversely not without God's ordination that it be done, as Scripture teaches. Similarly it is said elsewhere that the fact that the inhabitants of Gibeon opposed Israel was ordained by God who made their heart obstinate (Josh 11.20).

The way in which this happens is expressed by Scripture when in one passage God is said to have incited the angry heart of David to number the people (II Sam 24.1), while in another Satan is made the author of the incitement (I Chron 21.1). From this we understand that Satan is God's fan for impelling the hearts of men just as He pleases. This is said more explicitly elsewhere, where an evil spirit of the Lord enters Saul (I Sam 16.14ff.). Saul is certainly moved by his own criminality, and indulges his fury consciously and voluntarily. But none the less Satan impels him, and this with God not idly observing but actively willing. Elsewhere the Spirit of the Lord is said to be evil; and this must be improper, unless he is sent as minister and executioner of God's vengeance—the minister of the wrath of God not only in the sense of soliciting minds to evil cupidities, but of effectively drawing them. In this sense, Paul records error to be effectively and divinely sent, to make those believe a lie who were unwilling to obey the truth (II Thess 2.11). It is clear that not only is Satan by the command of God a lying spirit in the mouth of all the prophets, but his substitutes ensnare the reprobate so that they lose understanding and are drawn necessarily into error. What Paul says is to be understood in this way (Rom 1.28): those who are ungrateful to God, He gives over to a reprobate mind, and delivers them into foul and ignominious lusts, so that they do what is unspeakable and their bodies are outraged. We hear that, not by the permission of a quiescent God, but by His just judgment, they are abandoned to their lusts, for shamefully profaning His glory. How this happens, the passage itself states: God sent them an effective spirit of error. It is clear from this what conclusion must be drawn. The hand of God rules the interior affections no less than it superintends external actions; nor would God have effected by the hand of man what He decreed, unless He worked in their hearts to make them will before they acted. So Augustine's opinion is to be accepted:[1] When God wills to be done what cannot be done but by willing men, their hearts being so inclined that they will, He Himself effects this, not only by helping in their hearts but by determining them, so that, though they had no such intention, they fulfil what His hand and His counsel decreed. Even in the very elements of nature He wisely suggests this thought from which so many shrink.[2] For the great diversity in human talents to be observed,[3] since it is divinely implanted in them, is a splendid example of that secret working by which He rules and moves our hearts.

X.11. No mere permission in God

From this it is easy to conclude how foolish and frail is the support of divine justice afforded by the suggestion that evils come to be not by His will, but merely by His permission. Of course, so far as they are evils, which men perpetrate with their evil mind, as I shall show in greater detail shortly, I admit that they are not pleasing to God. But it is a quite frivolous refuge to say that God otiosely permits them, when Scripture shows Him not only willing but the author of them. Augustine conceded this to the accustomed and accepted forms of speech, for the time being; but when he proceeds farther to examine the thing more closely, he quite prohibits permission from taking the place of action. I shall not refer to all that he says about this matter in Book 5 of the *Contra Iulianum*. This will be enough:[4] These things He does in marvellous and ineffable ways, who knows how to execute His just judgments not only upon men's bodies but in their hearts; who does not make wills evil but uses them as He wills, while being Himself unable to will evil. Elsewhere in the same sense:[5] If diligently searched, Scripture shows not only the good wills of men, which He Himself made out of evil wills and are made good by Him, to be directed to good actions and to eternal life; even those which conserve the creatureliness of this world are so within the power of God, that He inclines them when He wills

---

[1] *De Praedest. Sanct.*, cap. 20.   [2] *De Peccat. Merit. et Remiss.*, lib. 1, cap. 22.

[3] French adds: some being fools, some stupid, some sharp, some prudent, some serious and some lightweight, etc.

[4] Cap. 3.   [5] *De Gratia et Libero Arbitr. ad Valent.*, cap. 20.

and as He wills, either to the enjoyment of benefits in the case
of some, or to the imposition of penalties in the case of others.
He adds:[1] Who does not tremble at these judgments with
which God works in the hearts of even the wicked whatever
He will, rewarding them none the less according to desert?
Again it is quite clear from the evidence of Scripture that God
works in the hearts of men to incline their wills just as He will,
whether to good for His mercy's sake or to evil according to
their merits, His judgment being sometimes open and sometimes
concealed, but always just. For it ought to be fixed in your
hearts that there is no iniquity with God. The reason recorded
for God's judgment being sometimes concealed is to be sought
in another passage.[2] Here he frequently declares that sins
are penalties which God justly returns upon those who had
first sinned; and then he rises to that higher and greater hidden
secret. God finds the material cause for exercising His wrath
in all except those whom He gratuitously elected. For, he says,
the rest of mortal men, who are not of that number, are born
of the same human race from which those come and are made
vessels of wrath for their benefit. For God creates none of them
rashly or fortuitously or because He did not know what good
He might work by them. For He effects this good, that in them
He creates a human nature and out of them He effects order
in the world.

The reason why He should sometimes fill the heart with
anxiety and fear and sometimes confirm it with courage, why
He should take away the spirit from princes and infatuate the
counsels of the wise, why He should bestow on some the spirit
of temperance and supply others with the spirit of wild fury—
the reason for all this He will one day make clear and conspicuous. But it will equally appear that His hidden judgment
is paramount, as He converts wills as seems good to Him. For
nature is common to all men, but not grace. So in another
place speaks the holy man.[3]

X.12. The will of God the necessity of all things

For the man who honestly and soberly reflects on these
things, there can be no doubt that the will of God is the chief
and principal cause of all things. It is fitting to restrain our

[1] Cap. 21.   [2] *Contra Iulianum*, lib. 5, cap. 7.
[3] *De Verbis Apostoli*, serm. 11.

minds by this knowledge, lest we pursue our investigations
beyond what is lawful. Augustine's word, that the will of God
is the necessity of things,[1] always seems at first hearing to be a
hard saying. But he adds[2] by way of explanation that God
made inferior causes in such a way that out of them that of
which they are the causes is possible but not necessary. But the
higher remote causes He hides in Himself, so that out of them
what He makes possible by them is necessary. To the man who
more attentively considers the matter, the harshness is easily
mitigated. For as he elsewhere says[3] in different words, the
facts and the meaning are wholly the same and they contain
in them no contradiction. God holds within Himself the
hidden causes of whatever is made, and these are not made
resident in created things. He gives effect to them not by the
operation of providence by which He upholds the nature of
things in being but as He administers them as He willed, so
He created them as He willed. Here is the grace by which
those are saved[4] who were lost.[5] For what is more true than
that God in ruling His creatures should hold hidden in Himself
more than He implanted in their natures? But of all the things
which happen, the first cause is to be understood to be His
will, because He so governs the natures created by Him, as to
determine all the counsels and the actions of men to the end
decreed by Him. Thus a limitation is imposed on us by this
doctrine which restrains us within the bounds of modesty, not
undeservedly, as I have said. For it is too absurd not to allow
existence to the will of God which is superior to all causes
unless His reason be apparent.

X.13. God's reasons

What I said earlier is to be borne in mind. God does nothing
without the best of reasons. But since the most certain rule of
righteousness is His will, it ought, as I may say, to be the
principal reason of all our reasonings. For the humility of
faith, as it is born out of a living reverence for the divine
righteousness, is no figment of ignorance.[6] For who that does

---

[1] *De Genes. ad Liter.*, lib. 6, cap. 15.   [2] Cap. 18.   [3] Ibid., lib. 9, cap. 18.

[4] So the chief authority alone; others have: are safe.

[5] French inserts: I pray you, what fault is to be found in these words?

[6] French has: a stupid ignorance which shuts the eyes to what Scripture shows
us.

not have the persuasion fixed deeply in his mind that God is righteous and all His works are right, can acquiesce simply in His good pleasure? Hence, I detest the doctrine of the Sorbonne, for which the papal theologicians applaud themselves, that invents for God an absolute power.[1] For it is easier to dissever the light of the sun from its heat, or for that matter its heat from fire, than to separate God's power from His righteousness. Let these monstrous speculations be put far away from pious minds, that God should be able to do more than is proper to Him or to act without rule or reason. Nor indeed do I accept the suggestion that, because God in doing anything is free from all law, He therefore is without censure. For to make God beyond law is to rob Him of the greatest part of His glory, for it destroys His rectitude and His righteousness. Not that God is subject to law, except in so far as He Himself is law. For such is the consent and agreement between His power and His righteousness, that nothing proceeds from Him that is not considered, legitimate and regular. And certainly the faithful both preach His omnipotence and necessarily acknowledge at the same time that He is judge of the world, so that they understand His power, in their meaning of the term, to be tempered with righteousness and equity.

X.14. God not the author of evil

But the objection is not yet resolved, that if all things are done by the will of God, and men contrive nothing except by His will and ordination, then God is the author of all evils. It is a true distinction that is current in the schools and is generally practised: rightly understood, the evil of punishment but not of guilt originates from God. Thinking that the difficulty here may be resolved by a single word, some are foolish enough serenely to overlook what occasions the greatest ambiguity; namely, how God may be free of guilt in doing the very thing that He condemns in Satan and the reprobate and which is to be condemned by men. For the work is the same, not different; and it is thought an evil on both sides, that praise for just punishment should necessarily be ascribed to God and blame to men. Robbers steal the cattle of the saintly Job. The deed is cruel and shameful. Satan by this means tempts him to desperation—an even more detestable machination.

---

[1] French adds: so as to be beyond law.

But Job himself indicates another author of the deed: The Lord gave, the Lord has taken away. He not unjustly transfers to God[1] what could not be attributed without the robbers. For, just as if he had witnessed with his eyes[2] what the story[3] narrates took place in the heavenly council, he confesses that God took away by the hands of plunderers what was none the less taken by His consent and authority. This he explains in the following words: As it pleased the Lord, so was it done. We learn then that the work was jointly the work of God and o Satan and of the robbers. We learn that nothing happens but what seems good to God. How then is God to be exempted from the blame to which Satan with his instruments is liable? Of course a distinction is made between the deeds of men and their purpose and end; for the cruelty of the man who puts out the eyes of crows or kills a stork is condemned, while the virtue of the judge is praised who puts his hand to the killing of a criminal. Why should the case of God be worse so that we may not distinguish Him in His justice from the misdeeds of men? To come to a closer analogy: the prince is praised who repels rapine and pillage from his borders in a just and legitimate war. For this purpose he will arm many soldiers whose lust to shed blood, to plunder the goods of the poor and for every kind of violent lawlessness are certainly not praiseworthy. Suppose that two armies engage in battle; suppose you discern in the general, under whose auspices and by whose command the battle is joined, an upright disposition though he be only a mortal man; do you not absolve him, while condemning the soldiers who set their hands to murder for shameful reward? and do you defraud God of the glory of His justice because He works by means of Satan? It comes to this: as the clouds which emanate from the earth obscure the splendour of the sun, so that it does not penetrate to the eyes of men, while the sun itself none the less remains resplendent, so the vanity of men gives rise to many impediments like vapours, which conceal the countenance of the divine righteousness, though it itself remain intact and unimpaired. This is what those do who wish to implicate God and the ungodly in an equal guilt. Not so David: when Shimei hurled insults and stones at him, he does not pass

---

[1] French has: In thus speaking, he does not wish to do injustice to God, nor to impute to Him a guilt which belongs to the brigands.

[2] French has: like an angel.   [3] French has: the Holy Spirit.

judgment upon the man himself, but considers the precept of
God: The Lord, he said, bade him curse (II Sam 16.11). Nor
did he revolt against God, but, humbly submitting his back to
the rod, he said: Who will dare to ask why this is done?
Similarly in the Psalm: I was silent, because thou has done it
(Ps 39.10). For what pious man is not reduced to silence by the
majesty of God? and from whom does His righteousness not
elicit a confession of praise? Surely he will break out in exclamation: Let him curse according to the precept of the Lord,
if only the Lord have respect to the affliction of His servant
(II Sam 16.11).

Hence, since the criminal misdeeds perpetrated by men
proceed from God with a cause that is just, though perhaps
unknown to us, though the first cause of all things is His will,
I nevertheless deny that He is the author of sin. What I have
maintained about the diversity of causes must not be forgotten:
the proximate cause is one thing, the remote cause another.
Then we shall know how great is the distinction between the
equitable providence of God and the stormy assaults of men.
Certain shameless and illiberal people charge us with calumny
by maintaining that God is made the author of sin, if His will
is made first cause of all that happens. For what man wickedly
perpetrates, incited by ambition or avarice or lust or some other
depraved motive, since God does it by his hand with a righteous
though perhaps hidden purpose—this cannot be equated with
the term sin. Sin in man is made by perfidy, cruelty, pride,
intemperance, envy, blind love of self, any kind of depraved
lust. Nothing like this is to be found in God. Shimei assaults
his king with monstrous petulance; and sin appears. God uses
this agent for the just humiliation of David, as a rod to chastise
him. Who accuses Him of sin? Arabs and Sabaeans carry off
booty from a stranger's goods. It is clearly the crime of pillage.
God exercises the patience of His servant by their violence.
There emerges from the whole affair the noble confession:
Blessed be the name of the Lord (Job 1.21), instead of audible
and sacrilegious complaints. In a word, such is the principle
with which God works in the sins of men, that when the
matter is referred to Him, He entirely removes every spot by
His purity.

Augustine has a useful admonition,[1] that, for all their

---

[1] *Enchir. ad Laur.*, cap. 101.

agreement here, there is a great difference between God and man. For God wills for good what men will for evil; and He does not will for good what men do not will for evil. So too, in their disagreement, men and God are not quite incongruous. For men will for good what God does not will for good; and they do not will for good what God does will for good. A son may wish for the death of his father, so that he may take over the inheritance; and God, too, may will that he die.[1] God willed that Jerusalem be destroyed, the temple profaned and pulled down to the foundations, and the Jews vexed with such extreme griefs; but the Idumeans wished for the same thing.[2] So that the stern and obstinate man who spares no one may have the same measure in the end measured to him, God does not will that any of his wealth be contributed when urgent need arises. The son may refuse every office of piety to his father, and be unwilling to support him. God did not will to supply wiser counsels to the sons of Eli, for it was decreed that he should lose them (I Sam 2.25); for they did not will to listen to their father. All this shows that there is from the beginning a kind of congruity; yet with respect to good and evil there is no less incongruity than between water and fire. The husband wishes for longer life for his wife, but God calls her from this world. Christ Himself shrinks and begs for deliverance from a death which was a sacrifice of the sweetest odour to God. The will of each, though differently orientated, is free of guilt. It is, then, not the case that God is to be included in the society of crime whenever some similarity appears between His hidden counsel and the manifestly vicious lusts of men. Augustine has this passage:[3] Therefore the great works of the Lord are contrived according to His desire, so that in a wonderful and ineffable way what is done against His will is yet not done beyond His will; for it would not be done did He not allow, and allow it not unwillingly, but willingly.

X.15. *God's nature and will are simple*

Thus is refuted the ignorance or wickedness of those who deny that the nature of God is single and simple, if another

---

[1] French adds: It may seem that there is agreement where there is only contradiction.

[2] French has: as is written in the Psalms (137.7).

[3] *Enchir. ad Laur.*, cap. 100.

will than that disclosed by Him in the law is attributed to Him.
Some in ridicule even ask, supposing there is a will of God not
revealed in the law,[1] how we are to call it. But they must
be crazy, if they dismiss the significance of so much scriptural
evidence,[2] which declares with admiration how profound are
the depths contained in the judgments of God. When Paul
exclaims: O the height and the depth! how inscrutable are His
judgments! (Rom 11.33), what he plainly teaches about the
judgment of God concerning the Jews is not different from what
is expressed in the words of Christ: O Jerusalem! how often
would I have gathered your chickens! (Mt 23.37; Lk 13.34).
In that Eli did not require his sons to be obedient to their
father, his will differed from the precept of the law by which
the son is required to be obedient to his parents. In a word,
whenever Scripture preaches the wonderful counsels and profound intentions of God, it speaks not of the precepts manifestly
put before our eyes, but praises that inaccessible light in which
His counsel is hidden, and so forces us more profoundly to
honour and adore, so far as our understanding permits.
Someone will say: If the light is inaccessible, how is there
access to it for us? But I do not accede to the demand to
investigate what God wills to hide far from inquisitive curiosity;
and whatever Scripture pronounces, I receive and embrace in
assured faith and reverence.[3] But how is it that God remains
perpetually identical with Himself, without any shadow of
turning (Jas 1.17), while yet willing something different from
what He manifests? I reply that it is no wonder if God in
speaking to men should accommodate Himself to their measure.
Who will say that God appears in visions as He really is? For
the splendour of His glory is such that its mere appearance
would rob us of all our senses. He therefore manifests Himself
as men are able to comprehend. For either God prattles with
us, or He veils what He knows to be incomprehensible to us,
though I deny that there is any pretence or deception in His
word. What the Psalm says (5.5) is very true, that God does
not willingly allow iniquity. This evidence from the mouth of

---

[1] supposing . . . —so the best reading found in the chief version following
Gallasius and French; Beza has the bad reading: if there is anything it is not
revealed; emended in Amst.: if there is anything which is not revealed.

[2] French adds: and so explicit.

[3] French adds: For it is not for us knowingly to ignore what God has willed to
teach us.

David is no different from what is in fact daily proved,[1] in that God exacts penalties on the sins of men. He would not punish if He did not hate. You see an avenger? —He certainly does not approve. Many go astray in not holding that God wills what men by sinning do. You ask how[2] He abominates incest and fornification. Is the deed of Absalom in publicly violating his father's concubine (II Sam 16.21) done with God unwilling? But He had Himself already predicted through His servant Nathan that He would do this: I shall take away your wives before your eyes, and give them to your neighbour to lie with them under this sun. Thou hast done it in secret, but I am about to do it in face of the whole people and under this sun (ibid., 12.11). Scripture is full of such examples.[3] Must we then impute the guilt of sin to God, or invent a double will for Him so that He falls out with Himself? I have shown that He wills the same as the criminal and the wicked, but in a different way. So now it is to be maintained that there is diversity of kinds while He wills in the same way, so that out of the variety which perplexes us[4] a harmony may be beautifully contrived. So far as Absalom's crime is a monstrous impiety against his father, a perfidious violation of a wife and a foul profanation of the order of nature, it certainly is displeasing to God; for He takes pleasure in honesty, chastity, good faith and modesty, and it is this order that He prescribes and wills to be obeyed and observed unimpaired among men. But because He is pleased to avenge the adultery of David in this way, He wills in the same way things that seem different to us.[5] For His will is single and simple, and by it He prescribes what ought to be done and also avenges transgressions of His law.[6] Elsewhere it is said that sins are the punishments which God exacts for previous sins. In such suggestions, there are two things to be taken into account. There is the righteous judgment of God by which He declares His hatred of sin and prescribes its penalty; and there is the wickedness of man which is apparently contrary to the will of God. Is it any wonder that such immense splendour should blunt the acuteness of our mind? Our physical eyes are not enough to sustain a contemplation of the

---

[1] French adds: by experience.   [2] Sentence omitted in versions.

[3] Sentence wanting in French edition.   [4] French has: which troubles us.

[5] French has: in the same way and in very close accord.

[6] French adds: In this God varies not at all.

sun. Is our spiritual insight greater than our natural powers, or the majesty of God inferior to the glory of the sun? It is becoming in us, then, not to be too inquisitive; only let us not dare to deny the truth of what Scripture plainly teaches and experience confirms, or even to suggest[1] that it does not reach agreement in God. When the last day dawns, as Augustine says,[2] there will be seen in the clear light of wisdom what pious faith now maintains before it is seen as manifest knowledge, namely, that the will of God is certain, immutable and most efficacious,[3] and that there are many things which it is able but does not will to do and nothing which it wills and is not able.

[1] French has: to keep nagging (literally: peck).
[2] *Enchir. ad Laur.*, cap. 95.
[3] French has: virtuous.

LAUS DEO

INDEX OF AUTHORS

PIGHIUS

ST AUGUSTINE

OTHERS

INDEX OF SCRIPTURAL PASSAGES

OLD TESTAMENT

APOCRYPHA

NEW TESTAMENT

NEW TESTAMENT—*cont.*